"*Grad to Grown-Up* is a must-read. What I learned from Gene about work ethic, respect, finance, and career helped get me to the NBA. Gene has the strongest character of anyone I know and a unique ability to build relationships with others. Every young person can learn from him, and this book is full of his invaluable insight."

—**Ryan Arcidiacono**, NBA player; 2016 Most Outstanding Player, Villanova University; previous RCI intern

"I'm betting on this book. It has all the elements of a bestseller! The interplay of a father's wise and practical advice and his daughter's good-hearted (and often funny) challenges make for a very readable set of informal business and financial commandments that any young person (or older person starting out on a new career) would be wise to follow."

—**Mark Morgan Ford**, Entrepreneur; *New York Times* bestselling author; President at Palimi, Inc.; CEO of Ford Fine Art

"I have known Gene and his family for over thirty-five years. Gene has had extraordinary success in both his professional and personal life. What I admire most about Gene is how he cares for and treats others. As a young professional, I reported to Gene, and he helped pave the path for me and others to be successful. Also, what he and his wife Michele do through their philanthropic activities is remarkable. I hope his book receives the attention it deserves, as there are many lessons others can benefit from."

—**Lloyd Erlemann**, Managing Director at Big Four Consulting Firm

"Want to be rich and enjoy your life, too? This book will get you there! I love the father-daughter approach. I wish my two daughters had this resource after graduating college—it has everything you need all in one place."

—**Robert Garzilli,** Former SVP at Salesforce.com; former Global VP of Sales at ServiceNow

"*Grad to Grown-Up* will help every person looking to grow and get on the path to success. It's these lessons that helped me achieve academic and personal success so young. Gene is a mentor to me to this day, and the book shares all his advice."

—**Dr. Kennedy Chukwuocha**, Doctor of Physical Therapy; previous RCI intern

"The wisdom in this book is timeless. Every young adult needs a GPS through life—the earlier the better!"

—**Dianna Booher**, Author of *Creating Personal Presence*
and Communicate with Confidence

"Gene is loved and admired by all who know him. He generously invests his time mentoring young people while encouraging them to reach their goals."

—**Julie Spencer**, Professional speaker; author of award-winning book
Looking Through a Keyhole

GRAD TO GROWN-UP

68 Tips to Excel in Your Personal and Professional Life

**GENE RICE &
COURTNEY BEJGROWICZ**

Post Hill
PRESS

A POST HILL PRESS BOOK

Grad to Grown-Up:
68 Tips to Excel in Your Personal and Professional Life
© 2022 by Gene Rice and Courtney Bejgrowicz
All Rights Reserved

ISBN: 978-1-63758-192-6
ISBN (eBook): 978-1-63758-193-3

Interior design by Greg Johnson, Textbook Perfect

Post Hill Press
New York • Nashville
posthillpress.com

Published in the United States of America
1 2 3 4 5 6 7 8 9 10

*This book is dedicated to my wife, who is the reason
for my success. There is no me without you.*

*And to my children, children-in-law, and grandchildren,
who inspired me to put my legacy into words.*

—GENE RICE

*I dedicate this book to my parents, who instilled the value
of family and fostered my passions.*

*To my husband, who supported me through this process,
and to our little boy, who sat in my arms, and then my lap,
and later at my feet while we created this work.
You both fill me with the deepest love.*

—COURTNEY BEJGROWICZ

CONTENTS

PART FIVE: Health and Relationships

ACKNOWLEDGMENTS

First, I want to thank my daughter, Courtney. Without her, this book never would have been published. She has been an inspiration to me since the day she was born. My nickname for her is Triple Threat because she is beautiful on the inside, beautiful on the outside, and the hardest worker I know. As a father, I could not be more proud of her accomplishments, but more importantly, of the person she is. Having her as my co-author made this venture extremely special.

I want to acknowledge my life partner, my motivation, and wife of thirty-eight years, Michele. Mish is my greatest supporter and encourages me in every one of my endeavors. This book would not have been possible without her. Not only did she watch our grandson while we worked, she edited every word. She was our third set of eyes, our voice of reason, and the source of many stories.

Thank you to my other three children Shannon, Makenzie, and Owen, my sons-in-law Douglas and Richard, my daughter-in-law Olivia, and my grandchildren Dylan, Emilia, Jacob, and Benjamin, and future generations. You have been the inspiration for this book. Without you, this project would never have been completed. It is the legacy I hope to pass on to all of you.

I would also like to acknowledge my parents and siblings. As the second oldest of six children, and the oldest boy, I realize my perception and experiences growing up might be different from theirs. My parents did the best they could and gave me the foundation to build the life I have today.

Lastly, I would like to recognize my business partner, Jeff Cohen, who left Alcatel with me to create Rice Cohen International. Without him, the firm never would have grown to what it is today. Thank you to all the interns I've worked with over the years and the executives that I have had the great pleasure of knowing and helping in their careers. I appreciate you sharing your lives with me and helping to inspire my life's work and this book.

Me and my legacy.

INTRODUCTION

> "If...there be any kindness I can show,
> or any good thing I can do to any fellow being,
> let me do it now, and not defer or neglect it,
> as I shall not pass this way again."

My deeper purpose is represented by this quotation often attributed to William Penn—I am called to help others whose paths I cross. My goal in writing this book is to share my life's learning so that you may find the happiness and success that brings you true fulfillment and utter joy. I hope to help you identify your passions and gifts to make them your life's work. I wish to help you mitigate the missteps and surmount the setbacks that you will face along the way. If you can use one idea to enhance your life, then I have achieved my goal. What I have learned from my successes and failures are now yours, too; I encourage you to claim them as your own and use them to help shape your journey.

Why You Should Read This Book

Some startling statistics about life in America:

- Student debt exceeds $1.4 trillion
- Credit card debt is over $1 trillion
- 37% of Americans would be at risk for living in poverty if they were without a job for three months
- 35% of adult children live at home

- Divorce rates have reached 50%
- The U.S. spends more money on healthcare than any
  other country

How is this possible in one of the wealthiest countries in the world, the land of opportunity?

If you are hoping to avoid becoming a statistic, this book is your roadmap to steer clear of the potholes. *Grad to Grown-Up* gives clear advice and guidance alongside real-life examples to help you achieve fulfillment.

Who Should Read This Book

The easy answer is everyone. I do believe this book has something to benefit anyone at any stage of life. But who comes to mind first? Graduates and young adults, specifically, my interns—brilliant interns from our nation's top colleges. I think of them because they have strong business skills but do not know how to invest in a 401(k). They are hardworking young adults who have one foot already on the hamster wheel of corporate America but cannot claim their jobs as vocations. For twenty years, I've sat with these interns weekly, sharing what became known as "Gene's Life Lessons" to help them prepare for the future, not just professionally, but personally. Those interns were my first audience. And now there is you!

This book is especially for those at the start of their careers, as well as those who are motivated to advance in their jobs and need the guidance to do so. This is for people who want to have success not just in business but in their personal lives too. This is for those who wish to live a more balanced, meaningful life.

Want to improve yourself? Be happier? More fulfilled? More successful? This book is for you.

Who I Am

I'm a rock 'n' roll club owner-turned-salesperson, then manager, then executive, and now business owner for over thirty years. I am a rags-to-riches story, from an immigrant family barely making ends meet to the regional manager overseeing all east coast operations at a division of Alcatel, an international Fortune 100 firm, by the age of thirty-two.

There, I was promoted five times in seven years and won the Executive of the Year award. I worked my way up the corporate ladder and am now an entrepreneur. I tell you this to show you that your dreams are possible. Like me, you can achieve success—I will help you get there.

My company, Rice Cohen International (RCI), quickly became one of the thirty largest and fastest growing search firms in North America. We are an executive retained search firm that specializes in building relationships with clients and candidates. In simpler terms, we are hired on retainer by companies to find the best talent to fill their senior-level positions. I have placed over one-thousand executives and interviewed tens of thousands of the top business leaders in the world. I know what exceptional talent looks like and what makes people successful. I understand the ins and outs of interviewing and how to get promoted. I train people on how to get the jobs of their dreams. I have the secrets, and I will share them with you.

I also hope to help you extend this success to your life at large. What has stood out to me the most in my experience is the executives who make well into six and seven figures aren't always happy. It seems that as they receive promotion after promotion, they get further away from the work they love. The most successful ones? They are passionate about what they do and find a greater purpose in life because of their work. They also find fulfillment outside the office. I have been blessed to have both in my life, and my wish is to help you accomplish the same.

My biggest achievement? It isn't my career success. It's growing my family and starting a nonprofit charity, the **Plant a Seed Inspire a Dream Foundation**, with my wife of thirty-eight years. All my personal profits from this book will go to the charity, which supports the passions of underserved youth.

What's Inside

This book is divided into five sections: Life, Job Search, Career, Personal Finance, and Health and Relationships. Each section will present multiple chapters that offer insight into a particular area of your life and share ideas to improve it.

Every page is written with you in mind. There are stories, examples, charts, statistics, and quotations to illustrate the information so that it's relatable and easy to comprehend. The chapters are straightforward but make you think, and hopefully they keep you inspired and laughing.

To be more inclusive and avoid wordiness and confusion, I use plural pronouns throughout instead of singular when discussing different scenarios and giving examples. I also change the names of specific people to protect their privacy.

Beware, there is a shift in style and tone when you move from sections one through four into section five, Health and Relationships. You will not achieve the professional life of your dreams without tending to your personal life, and section five is devoted to the most intimate parts of the personal. To do it justice, I peel back layers and divulge parts of my past and present that are difficult to share. This was the most challenging section to write, but I hope that the vulnerability inspires your own growth and reflection.

It is the nature of this book to present short chapters, so section five does not develop each personal tip in depth. I cannot do justice to some of the personal topics, such as leaving your baggage behind, in just a few pages. I share resources at the end of some of the chapters in case you wish to explore the subject further.

Last but certainly not least, each chapter concludes with commentary from my third born. That's the best part—I wrote this book with my thirty-two-year-old daughter, Courtney. CJ, as I call her, keeps me honest, relevant, and focused. I am excited for you to hear her genuine and personal voice alongside mine. Her commentary offers a youthful perspective. Like you, Courtney is newly navigating adulthood and wishes to find success and purpose.

Courtney graduated from Lehigh University with two bachelor's degrees, one in English and one in economics, as well as a Master of Education. She currently teaches high school English and has a passion for helping others. She takes my advice and relates it to jobs beyond the business sector, offering her unique viewpoint as someone working outside of corporate America. She is a new wife, new mother, and juggling many responsibilities while forging her path into adulthood, and you will find her humor, added tidbits, openness, and stories engaging. Depending on the topic, her role shifts. She transforms from your honest best friend to my sarcastic daughter, to an insightful intellectual, to your personal cheerleader, to your very own researcher. Her commentary often takes center stage in section five as she pushes me to examine life and difficult topics from many perspectives.

Our voices side-by-side will keep you engaged, laughing, and learning.

How to Approach This Book

You can try to Google all sorts of topics, but you don't know what you don't know—you need to start somewhere. That somewhere is here. If you want to read the book cover-to-cover, you might try reading one or two chapters a day. But you do not have to read it in order. You might start with the job search section if you are focused on finding a new position, or the career section if looking to advance professionally. You might even want to start with the last chapter! This book is built to be read in any order that serves your needs.

We hope you keep going back to this book with each life stage and decision. We envision you rereading a chapter when a situation arises. Getting your annual physical? Read the chapter about being an active participant in your healthcare. Buying or leasing a car? Revisit that chapter first. Heading out on an interview? Read the five-step interview preparation process again. Getting married? Peruse the chapter about sharing finances as a springboard for critical discussion with your partner.

We hope this book is the gift that keeps on giving. Write in the book. Think alongside it. Come back to it often. And then pass it on!

We wish you happiness and blessings as you work through these chapters and take control of your own life. And congratulations on choosing YOU.

COURTNEY COMMENT

My dad is like the Genie from *Aladdin*. Wishes? He can't grant them out of thin air, but he will do everything in his power to make your dreams come true. He's your sage best friend with a heart of gold. He always shows up. Simply put, he's larger than life. And he's quality comic relief, too.

Sure, he's human and imperfect, but he's the most amazing imperfect human I know. He brings magic wherever he goes. He's the Genie without the lamp and flying carpet.

My dad's stories in this book are genuine and his advice pure (believe me, I called him out on any BS and deleted it—I have your back!). I am so excited to share him with you. To know him and learn from him is to love him, and when you are done reading this book, I know that you will.

What does it mean to learn from my dad?

When I was eleven, I had a chinchilla. Joey lived in my room in a way-too-tiny pen that broke my heart. One day, I saw what I would call the Ritz Carlton of chinchilla cages at PetSmart and needed to have it. There were four levels, hammocks, and tunnels galore. But my dad wouldn't buy it.

He explained that when we love something, we work hard to provide for it. He committed to paying for half the cage, but I would have to earn the money to pay for the rest. I spent the next two months weeding in the garden and picking up extra chores. In the end, Joey got his Taj Mahal, and I learned the value of a dollar. And self-respect. And love.

This story recently came to me as I planned for my son's first birthday. I wanted to give him the most epic Wild One dinosaur party and went Pinterest mom crazy to do so. I shopped for months to find the perfect décor, food, and gifts. But when the celebration was over, I thought, *How am I going to give him the gifts he really needs?* How do I teach him the value of money, love, and work ethic? These are the things adults need to think about! Panic attack, commence.

I am sure I am not alone in having these *Holy crap, I'm an adult!* moments. They seem to get more and more frequent these days.

Fortunately, life is a beautiful cycle. I can create my own teachable moments (hopefully rodent-free) because I had the best dad to learn from.

And now you get to have him too. Growing up and becoming independent adults is freaking hard! Like you, I'm smack in the middle of it.

But this book is like a survival guide, and we'll navigate the rocky waters of adulthood together with my dad (and maybe some wine?) leading us through.

Remember, deep breaths. We can do this.

Happy reading!

PART ONE

LIFE

1

What's Your Foundation?

The greatest masterpieces in the world all began with their foundations. Without them, the structures would crumble—the Statue of Liberty would sink into the sea and the Leaning Tower of Pisa would finally fall. The same is true for human beings. Without your principles and beliefs, you have no direction; you cannot build your life without a strong base.

The younger you are when you identify your foundation, the easier it is to make critical life decisions and grow as a human being. Aristotle said it best: "Knowing yourself is the beginning of all wisdom." When you understand what drives and motivates you, you can take control of your own path in life. Begin by asking yourself, **What are my values?**

This driving question can be asked in many ways. *What is the foundation upon which I want to build? From where do I pull my inspiration? What thoughts and opinions spark the most fire?* You must dig deep within yourself to discover your strongest passions and influences. Is it family? God? Friendship? Is it your health? Your country and the freedoms provided? Trust and honesty? Is it a strong belief in helping the underserved?

Your foundation must be just that—yours—not dictated by anyone else, even your parents (although what you learn from them might be a good place to start). Knowing your core values will shape the life you create and help you navigate hardships.

I first became aware of the importance of a foundation when mine was questioned. I was at a crossroads, which is often when foundations are most important. I grew up on Long Island in a religious, blue-collar family. I attended Catholic School my entire education and served as an altar boy in church. As the eldest son in my Irish Catholic family, becoming a priest would have been the greatest honor to my parents.

Then the most beautiful girl walked into my life. Well, she walked into my bar. This little Jewish hippie took my life by storm. We were both anomalies: Michele, a free spirit working as a speech therapist in a school, and me, a Catholic schoolboy owning a rock 'n' roll club. Our hearts aligned, and more importantly, our values were in sync.

Could I really marry someone who wasn't Catholic? My mom believed I shouldn't.

"Knowing yourself is the beginning of all wisdom."

—ARISTOTLE

Me? When I thought about it, I knew I could; actually, I had to. And making this decision helped me identify and act on my core principles at twenty-six years young. My foundation was the compass I needed to make this colossal decision, and it was the best one I ever made (and lucky for me, she said "yes!").

What is most important to me? The answer to this question was the same then as it is now:

1. Family, specifically marriage and children
2. Giving back
3. Work ethic
4. Kindness and understanding
5. Continuous learning

Religion is not on my list. It was on my parents' lists, and though spirituality is important to me, I realized organized religion is not personally a deal-breaker. What is critical, my number one value, is family, and I was certain Mish was the person to build that with. We share core principles, and, to me, that supersedes any religious differences. Plus, our religions weren't erased. My wife respected my desire to take our kids to church on Sundays, and we celebrated the Jewish holidays as a family. My kids loved it because they received Christmas and Hanukkah gifts, and more importantly, they were exposed to diverse cultures.

Without my values, I wouldn't have what I have today. I built this fulfilling life of mine from the foundation up.

So, take a minute to ask yourself: ***What do I stand for?***

And, who knows, finding the answer might just help you meet your own Jewish hippie who keeps your world from crumbling day in and day out.

COURTNEY COMMENT

The younger, hipper half of this duo is chiming in to remind you that most people don't think about these things. But you are special. You bought this book. You want to have more purpose and meaning in your life.

So, sit down tonight and pour yourself a glass of wine, ask Alexa to shuffle some acoustic coffeehouse music, and invest in yourself. Ask yourself the above questions. Jot down some answers. Give yourself time to figure it out. Hey, if my dad never did this, I wouldn't be here to guide you! Your answers matter, and they will shape your life.

2

Seek Out the Oldest Person in the Room

Never miss an opportunity to sit with, listen to, and learn from someone who is your senior. Our country hasn't placed enough value on the aging population (and no, I'm not saying this because I am now officially a member of AARP). Many people in our country fight getting older, buying rejuvenation creams and dressing half their age. But this isn't the case everywhere. In India, the eldest are the heads of the family. In China, it's an honor to have a grandparent live with you, and you're socially stigmatized if you send your parents to a nursing home. In Korea, elders are the authority figures. And in Greece, if you call someone "Old Man," it's a term of respect, not used to poke fun.

**Our elders deserve to be treated
with the utmost deference.**

What do these cultural differences teach us? We're doing it wrong. Our elders deserve to be treated with the utmost deference. Tap into their knowledge and learn from their pasts.

Some of the greatest life lessons will come from the wisdom of your elders. I often think of Papa Butch, a neighbor's father who I was blessed to spend late nights with on my front porch. He told me about his time in World War II and his regrets of spending days away from his family while on the road as a truck driver. As a young father, I valued these lessons that helped shaped me into who I am today.

Whenever possible, include seniors, and watch the positive impact it has on everyone. When I coached my son's AAU basketball team, we involved the grandparents. Two of the grandfathers came to almost all our practices and games. Grandpa Jack was an ex-FBI agent under J. Edgar Hoover and always had an enthralling story to share. He often told the boys that "Profanity is the weapon of the witless." If any of my players cursed in practice, they would be sent over to Grandpa Jack for a lesson on language until he determined they were ready to play again. It did not take long before we were a swear-free team. This helped the players gain more respect from the referees, our opponents, and most importantly the college coaches looking to recruit them.

Grandpa Harold, the other grandfather, is a jokester who loved the team camaraderie. One time he went on the road with us to Las Vegas, and I brought him in to pump the boys up with a pre-game speech. They circled around him as he screamed words of encouragement, and our players were bouncing off the ceiling by the end of the huddle. The team grandparents loved being included, but I think the ones who benefited the most were my players. From Grandpa Jack, they learned self-respect and discipline. From Grandpa Harold, they learned compassion and humor. From all the grandparents, they learned unconditional love and support.

I encourage you to always seek out the oldest person in the room wherever you go and engage in conversation. Introduce yourself, ask the proper questions, and listen. Not sure what to ask? Try one of the following:

- What lessons can I learn from you that might be helpful in my life?
- Do you have any regrets?
- What advice would you give to your eighteen-year-old self?
- What world events do you remember most vividly?
- What's the secret to a long and happy life?

I wish for you the wisdom and guidance that only an elder can bring—they are real-life historians. Embrace those that came before you, respect them, and honor them. It won't be too long before you're in their shoes.

COURTNEY COMMENT

What have you learned from the elders in your family? I encourage you to get your history from them before it's too late!

One of my favorite trips was to Castle Blaney, Ireland where my grandfather grew up. I never met my grandfather, but I felt him come alive there. His brother, Felix, was still living at the family's farm, and we visited with his sister, Delia, too (my great uncle and great aunt). I soaked up every moment I could with them to learn about my past, their lives, and their wisdom.

I went back to my hotel room each night and wrote down all the stories they shared—how my great grandfather barged into the school to defend Aunt Delia, and how the family couldn't all fit at the table so some of the kids ate on the steps. I learned about how they walk the cattle into town, still, to sell, and about the "raise the roof" farm parties.

What I was actually learning was where I came from, the Rice family work ethic, and love. I am so happy I spent those late nights by the fire asking questions and listening (deciphering Uncle Felix's post-Guinness brogue was definitely worth it).

Who and what do you come from? What can you learn from your own real-life historians?

3

It's Never Too Early to Start Making a Difference

It's important to make a positive impact on the world. In my life, I have seen how social media amplifies marginalized voices, highlights inequities, and mobilizes movements. Facebook even encourages users to hold birthday fundraisers, asking friends to donate to a cause instead of giving a gift. GoFundMe pages frequently raise thousands for people in need. We live in a time when spreading awareness happens at lightning speed, and money can be raised all over the world from the comfort of your home.

With so many opportunities to make an impact and give back to your community, where do you start? Like everything else I preach, begin with passion! What causes are personal to you? What do you care about most? What skills do you have that could help others? Have you lost a loved one to breast cancer? Did illiteracy impact your upbringing? Do you have a friend battling PTSD after returning home from war? If you give back in a way that's meaningful to you, you'll be more invested in the cause.

My middle daughter has always been passionate about animals. She loved horseback riding, had a pet shop mural painted on her bedroom wall, and brought home injured creatures regularly. In her adult life, she uses this passion to help rehabilitate wildlife. She volunteers at Aark Wildlife Rehabilitation and Education Center to nurse animals back to health and reintroduce them to their habitats. She helps at their fundraisers and aids in their education efforts. She even brought home twenty-seven ducklings once! When service is a passion, it's a gift to not only those on the receiving end but also to yourself.

Some of my best memories come from the times I volunteered. What's great about volunteering? You don't need anything more than your time and energy to help others. When Michele and I had little money to give, we held an annual three-on-three basketball tournament with friends to raise money for the Make-A-Wish Foundation, a charity close to our hearts that grants wishes to children with life-threatening illnesses. Beyond fundraising, we had the opportunity to meet with the children, accompany them on outings as their wishes were granted, and run some of Children's Hospital of Philadelphia's BINGO nights for the hospitalized kids. On the car rides home, Michele and I would be overwhelmed and inspired by the children's courage and generosity: in *every* case that the hospitalized child won BINGO, they chose a prize for a friend or family member rather than themself. Seeing that ignites something in you.

Sharing your skills is another wonderful way to give back. Habitat for Humanity is an organization that builds or renovates affordable housing. The family that will be living in the home works alongside volunteers to build their house. My company took two workdays to volunteer on one of these projects. Everyone was able to add value, but my staff with carpentry skills were extra helpful. What are you good at? Is there anyone in need who could benefit from those skills?

**"We can't help everyone,
but everyone can help someone."**

—RONALD REAGAN

You can certainly make monetary donations or donate goods to help others in need as well. I caution you to do your research before donating because not all charities are created equal. If you're not careful, you might unknowingly donate to a scam or a cause you don't agree with. Make sure your donations go to a legal charity and check their vision and mission statements before donating to ensure they align with your values. I also recommend looking at what percentage of your donation actually goes to the cause. For example, Big Brothers/Big Sisters of America (National Office) does a wonderful job and uses 91% of their funds on charitable programs, and it costs them only seven dollars to raise one hundred.[1]

Coming together under a common goal builds a sense of community. Regardless of where you focus your service, it's important to leave the planet a better place. Improving one person's life can change their world and yours. As Ronald Reagan said, "We can't help everyone, but everyone can help someone." And that someone matters.

COURTNEY COMMENT

My dad's words in this chapter remind me of a quotation often attributed to Ralph Waldo Emerson: "To leave the world a bit better, whether by a healthy child, a garden patch, or a redeemed social condition; to know that even one life has breathed easier because you have lived—that is to have succeeded." Success expands much further than personal attainment. Our service to others matters a lot, and small acts have impact. Kindness matters.

I had a student who spent many lunch hours in my classroom. It was not always easy to give up my class-free time to help her, but I knew she needed the extra attention and encouragement. Sometimes I simply provided a quiet space to eat or safe space to read while I graded papers. Other times we discussed her goals and dreams.

I never thought much of it until three years later when she came back to visit. She wanted to thank me for all the extra time and effort. She was proud to share she had moved from my remediation class to an honors English class years later. She was also excited to be thinking about college. What had been some lunchtime chats to me and a little of my time helped this student believe in her abilities. How could so little mean so much? I am not sure—I just know that it did!

---

[1] "Top Rated Charities," CharityWatch, last updated 2020, https://www.charitywatch.org/top-rated-charities. Last accessed July 28, 2021.

I tell this story to remind you that you never know how your actions and time will impact others. Giving back comes in many different forms, and it does not have to be through a formal organization or event. It starts with being kind to others and giving a little of yourself. Your world will be better for it.

4

There's No Success Without Failure

Failure is the essence of success. We hear it often. Thomas Edison claims he failed one-thousand times before inventing the light bulb. Michael Jordan was cut from his high school basketball team before dominating the NBA. Winston Churchill had to repeat a year in primary school before becoming one of the most notable prime ministers in England's history. Henry Ford went bankrupt five separate times before finding success with the automobile. The examples are endless, but the message is the same: failure is just a step (or most likely multiple steps) on the journey to achievement. Embrace it!

If you let failure destroy you, it destroys your potential. It destroys your prospects. It destroys your future. Failure is an opportunity! Without my "epic fail," as my grandchildren would call it, I would not be where I am today.

At twenty-two years old, I managed and owned a rock 'n' roll club. I made more money as a young kid than my dad did as a steamfitter in New York supporting a family of eight. Life was a party, literally. I felt invincible. My club was the hottest in town, offering all original live music and theme nights. I was on top of the world.

Until I wasn't. Like many young people who find success early, I took it for granted. I became resentful of one of my partners who wasn't present day-to-day, and I gave him an ultimatum: sell me his share or I'm gone. Of course, it backfired, and I left to open my own bar. I was young and dumb. The bar I left had the best bands, an established following, and a small police force that protected it. It took me a year on my own to find a location and get a liquor license. I opened my bar in the jurisdiction of a large police force where the neighbors complained about the noise and we racked up violations. I had to borrow money from my future wife to pay the electric bill. I couldn't make ends meets, and I moved on from there, feeling like the biggest loser.

But what I thought was an "epic fail" actually led to my "epic win"— my business career, my family, and my work ethic. After this setback, I never again took success for granted. I learned to cherish and appreciate a good thing when I had it. I would never again be impulsive; instead, I now make calculated moves. These lessons propelled me forward and instilled an insatiable drive to do better.

I have seen many people struggle with failure. But I challenge you to reframe the commonly held belief that failure is the end. Instead, think of it as an intermission, an experience that allows you to try again with more information. When faced with a misstep, I implore you to ask:

1. What part did I play in the misstep?

Take responsibility for the failure. Don't point the finger. If you cannot take ownership of it, you can't reap the benefits of the success that can follow.

2. What could I have done differently?

This is where you gather information. If you can learn from the mistake, you will have more insight the next time a similar situation presents itself.

3. What now?

Real failure is making the same mistake twice. If you move forward and keep trying, you have not failed. Don't be defeated. Don't let the devastation derail you; let it fuel you!

**Don't let the devastation derail you;
let it fuel you!**

When you face defeat, you are one step closer to a better outcome. And you're in great company!

COURTNEY COMMENT

Failure and resilience go hand-in-hand. Resilience is the ability to bounce back; it's a muscle that builds over time, strengthening with each setback you overcome. Resilient people are better equipped for "adult" life because they can rebound more quickly from obstacles.

I did not have to flex that resilience muscle much as a child. One of the biggest perceived failures of my childhood was getting cut from the 9th grade basketball team. I left practice crying hysterically, and my dad felt awful. His reaction? He went in and talked to the coach, who then offered to let me join the team as an alternate. I'm mortified, looking back. I decided to stick with volleyball instead, but this is a microcosm of my upbringing.

My parents wanted to soften the blow at every turn. And I get it. With my son, I actually have to repeat, *let him fall*, then grit my teeth as I step aside. Rather than trying to erase the failures, it would have served me to learn how to face them head-on because a failure-free life is nonexistent.

As an adult, I have been turned down for a job, broken up with, and endured potholes galore. How have I handled such setbacks? Not very well! I can be overly sensitive and fragile. My gut reaction is to avoid and resist failure. I don't think I'm alone in this—it seems to be a common trait of our generation. Unfortunately, fighting failure is not serving us well because adulthood is naturally fraught with hurdles.

The solution? Give yourself opportunities and grace to build your resilience muscle. As I learn resilience, I get stronger, and it is easier to face and embrace each obstacle. Life is much smoother when I accept the hurdles than when I try to avoid them altogether. You can learn to do the same by following the steps my dad outlined and keep on keeping on.

5

You're Always Right

The power of positive thought is preached far and wide by doctors, pastors, and teachers alike. Your thoughts matter, and they don't just impact your reality—they create it.

The way your brain works supports this idea. Brain connections are primed to see, react, and form networks based upon your beliefs. For example, if you believe no one will ever love you, your brain functions based upon that premise. If five people profess their love for you while one abandons you, your brain reacts to the one person who reinforces the belief that you are not worthy of love and filters out all the others who challenge it. Your brain will reinforce your concept of self. Henry Ford explained it best: "Whether you believe you can do a thing or not, you are right."

Take the placebo effect, for example. Pain patients were unknowingly given sugar pills to see the impact on their suffering. The finding? The belief alone that they were receiving treatment was enough to reduce real physical pain even though there was no actual treatment.

I experienced the positive power of my thoughts firsthand. When my bar began to fail, I decided it was time to get out of the industry. That's when I entered the sales world. I was determined to make a corporate career happen. I could see it; I could feel it. I never even entertained a reality where I would not succeed. Michele and I sat down with *The New York Times* every night, circling job postings and talking with recruiters. I reached out to mentors, built up my resume, and dressed the part thanks to my father-in-law who bought me my first suit. I became the businessman I knew I was before I even had the job. I was then hired for my first sales job at a division of Alcatel to sell shipping equipment, and I was going to be the best salesperson they ever had. My thoughts never strayed from that vision.

At that first sales job, my territory was challenging, but my brain processed the challenge as an opportunity. I did not focus on the negatives and instead conjured up creative ways to make sales—befriending the UPS delivery providers in my area to learn which companies shipped the most packages, presenting the product in an innovative way, and offering selective discounts. I had a lofty quota, but I was committed to exceeding it. I had the skills; I had the capability; I certainly had the drive. What happened? Exactly what I envisioned. I was promoted within thirteen months and eventually managed the entire east coast.

**"Whether you believe you can
do a thing or not, you are right."**

—HENRY FORD

I later learned that the five previous people in my territory had failed miserably. What made me different? It clearly wasn't my experience or even my skill. Anyone can befriend a UPS driver. My superpower was my belief in myself. I found a way because I did not let failure enter the realm of possibility. Going back to the bar business wasn't an option. Where the salespeople before me saw a dry territory with no hope, I saw potential. Rather than obsess over a fear of failing, I obsessed over succeeding. And so that's what was manifested.

You have this superpower, too, if you choose to harness it. Your beliefs are a self-fulfilling prophecy, and your achievements will stem from your confidence in your abilities. I challenge you to confront your inner critic and foster your inner cheerleader. Remember, either way you're right.

COURTNEY COMMENT

Growing up, my dad always told me I could be whatever I wanted to be. He would insist I could be a WNBA player or the first female president if I put my mind to it. His belief in me was grandiose and bigger than my belief in myself. I'm five-foot-three-inches and chubby with bad knees—this girl was never making it to the WNBA. But the message was clear: with a good work ethic, I will be successful. Positive thoughts lead to positive action, which reaps positive results.

So, no, my dad is not claiming that if you think nonstop about winning the lottery then you will win (although some people claim they really did manifest their million-dollar wins). Your mind is powerful, but it's not magic. What he does believe is that your beliefs affect your reality, and I believe that's worth a shot!

6

Become a Continual Learner

"Did you learn anything new today?" This is the question I asked my children every night and now ask my grandchildren to nurture curiosity from a young age. On a smaller scale, learning daily tidbits stretches your mind and fosters creativity and discussion. On a larger scale, it helps you continue to grow as a person and challenge your prejudices; inquisitiveness impedes ignorance. If you remain open-minded, there is an opportunity at every turn to discover something new about yourself, your community, and the world.

I attribute much of my success to my love for learning. In the past five years, I have taken up the drums and chess, watched countless documentaries, read numerous books, took a course for new authors, and consumed news from all sides of the political spectrum. I keep learning and therefore growing, even in my sixties. There is always more to discover!

I remain ignorant in many areas, and as a white man in America, I am working to learn more about the experiences of marginalized groups. I used to proudly proclaim, "I'm not racist. I don't even see color!" I now understand that those were uninformed, detrimental comments. I should have been working toward being an anti-racist with a profound respect for diverse races and experiences. I should have been pushing myself to call out racism in everyday life and support minority-owned businesses. I should have been listening! How did this change come about? Continual learning!

I was given feedback that understanding my own implicit biases was how I could support fighting racism in our country and was handed the book *How to Be an Antiracist* by Ibram X. Kendi. After reading the book, attending a live talk, and listening to others' experiences, I understand that acknowledging my power and privilege is extremely important. I also know I have a lot more listening and learning to do. But I am growing and changing. I used to avoid conversations about racism with friends or family that have differing views. Now? I go there. You can't shy away from the difficult conversations if you want to grow.

**Everything is an opportunity
to discover something new.**

Further, your learning will benefit you most when it's meaningful. My eight-year-old grandson Dylan is incredibly bright, and I worry that boredom could extinguish his love for learning. I always ask what he's recently learned to help keep that fire lit. If he claims he hasn't learned anything new, I take on the challenge to help him, and he is thankfully still eager for me to do so. During one of these times, I asked if he knew the name of the highest mountain in the world. Without missing a beat, he responded, "Easy! Mount Everest. Did you know it's not the tallest, just the highest?" And then he went on to teach me about ocean mountain ranges and share trivia about ventures up the mountain. This wasn't the first time my fun fact didn't stump him, and I was the one doing the learning. But I wouldn't let an opportunity to foster growth pass us by.

So I asked a simple question: "Where is Mount Everest?" You could tell he was baffled and knew he overlooked the obvious. He could recite the name of the mountain and numerous fun facts, but he couldn't place it in the world. There was no application to his knowledge. I was able to teach him something after all: Mount Everest is in Nepal and Tibet, and I also pointed them out on our globe. More importantly, I reminded him that knowledge is nothing if not applicable.

To foster curiosity, you can simply push yourself to discover one new thing every day, take up a new hobby, or learn from a peer. Who knows where that could lead you?

Try one of the following:

- Listen to podcasts and TED Talks (free on the app)
- Play games on the Duolingo app to learn a new language
- Type "fact of the day" in Google for random trivia
- Use the dictionary.com app to learn a new word every day
- Use Flipboard to browse news articles of interest
- Keep a book by your bedside and read for five minutes a night
- Watch a documentary or educational channel such as Discovery
- Use the Magoosh test-prep. app to learn specialized material
- Find something easy to implement daily.

I wish you a lifetime dedicated to the pursuit of knowledge and growth so that you never become stagnant. Just remember not to get so lost in the quest that you lose sight of the horizon.

COURTNEY COMMENT

I would drown as a teacher if I hadn't grown up with parents that fostered inquiry.

Teaching is always changing. There will continually be new books, new technology, new philosophies, and new methods to enhance my craft. It is my love for learning that allows me to stay ahead of the trends (and it is this passion for knowledge that I hope to instill in my students).

As young people, keeping up with ever-changing trends and technology comes naturally to us. We should own this strength! We're not stuck in our ways and are ready to take on new ideas, and platforms, with vigor. Use that to your advantage, especially in your career.

I was able to present different applications to my colleagues from an early stage in my profession because I had a degree of technical expertise. Staying on top of teaching trends helped me excel in my career. Don't miss the opportunity to have it do the same for you. Discovered a resource that helps you be more efficient at work? Inquire if you can formally share it with your team!

Curiosity might have killed the cat, but it definitely saved the human!

7

Personalize Goal Setting

Research proves that appropriate goal setting leads to increased motivation, focus, and energy. I first began setting goals in my professional life, which then transferred into my personal one. It is a habit that persists to this day and one that I attribute my accomplishments to.

I was never formally taught how to set goals. Like all great persisting habits, it was born from need. As a young person starting out in business, there was a great deal I wanted to accomplish, and I needed a way to keep track of it all. In my early days, I wrote lists. My coworkers poked fun at me because these scribbled to-dos were found all over my desk and books.

My to-do lists graduated into a personal goal-setting system. I record long-term goals in my journal at the start of each year, and every Sunday to this day I write my short-term weekly goals (professional, personal, and financial) in a notebook and then pin them to my monitor where I will see them multiple times a day. Who can procrastinate when your goals are in front of your face screaming to be completed?

Beyond their physical placement, the content of your goals is essential. Goals should be:

- **Realistic:** They can be accomplished
- **Motivating:** They challenge you (you're proud when they're completed)
- **Measurable:** You know how close you are to completing them and exactly when they're accomplished
- **Recorded:** They are written down

This last point is the game changer and an integral part of my process. If goals are not written down, they are simply wishes. A study conducted on adults in the workplace ranging in age from twenty-three to seventy-two found that when people recorded and shared their goals, 76% achieved them compared to only 43% who didn't record and share them.[2] Writing and communicating your goals increases your focus and accountability.

**You must know what you're working toward
before being able to attain it.**

Having goals in my own handwriting and reviewing them daily helps me own them. Being able to check them off once completed makes me feel accomplished. Completing your goals has an impact beyond finishing the task itself—it leads to increased satisfaction, self-confidence, independence, and further motivation.[3]

If you want to achieve success and juggle all of life's responsibilities, goal setting is a crucial practice. Find a method that works for you and personalize it. You must know what you're working toward before being able to attain it.

---

[2] Sarah Gardner and Dave Albee, "Study focuses on strategies for achieving goals, resolutions," *Dominican Scholar*, February 1, 2015, https://scholar.dominican.edu/news-releases/266/. Last accessed July 28, 2021.

[3] Edwin A. Locke, "Toward a theory of task motivation and incentives," *Organizational Behavior And Human Performance 3*, no. 2 (May 1968): 157-189, https://www.sciencedirect.com/science/article/abs/pii/0030507368900044. Last accessed July 28, 2021.

COURTNEY COMMENT

In education, we teach goal setting ad nauseam; most students groan audibly at very mention of it by the time they reach high school. SMART goals, anyone?

So, what makes my dad's message different? I think it is the fact that his goal setting is non-academic in nature. He writes his goals in short-hand, keeps them simple, and makes them very personal. There are some guidelines but no rules (or teachers) making you use checklists, full sentences, and detailed action steps. And it only takes five minutes a day to think, reflect, and check in on what needs to be done.

To bring this practice into the twenty-first century (although I am still a huge fan of physically writing and posting goals), you might consider using the **notepad app** in your phone to record and store your goals and then set reminders in your calendar to reflect on them daily. Or maybe a checklist app such as **Clear** would work best for you since it makes it easy to sort your items and it is fun to swipe them away when complete. Or how about trying those cute digital post-it notes you can pin to your desktop home screen? The possibilities are endless! You just need to find the method that works best for you.

8

Know Your Linchpin

The word linchpin comes from the 1300s and refers to a pin that is passed through the end of an axel to keep a wheel in position. If the linchpin is removed, the wheel detaches. In more recent times, linchpin refers to a person in an organization who is indispensable and essential to the group's functionality. In both cases, a linchpin holds everything together and keeps things in working order.

**Prioritizing the activities you love...
is not selfish; it's essential.**

Metaphorically, your linchpin is the regular activities you need to do to stay grounded. Without these, you would fall apart, just like the wheel without the pin or the group without its organizer. Knowing what you need to do every single day or week to stay centered will help you avoid burnout and stay on top of your physical and mental wellbeing.

For me, no matter how crazy life gets, if I exercise, meditate, eat healthy, read, and spend time with my family, I am okay and can persevere through the curveballs. The less time I dedicate to these activities, the more likely I am to react impulsively or think negatively. For my son, his linchpin is golf (and more golf). If he can escape to the course at least once a week and clear his head, he can be effective in his day-to-day life no matter the stress.

We live in a society where people literally work themselves to death. My father was a steamfitter who called out of work only twice in his entire lifetime. He was defined by his job and had no other healthy activities to help him unwind. The day he passed away, he wasn't feeling well but insisted on going in anyway. Later, he had a massive, fatal heart attack in the parking lot of work. I never saw him alive again.

Many people work, sleep, and do little in between. But when you become so busy juggling your career and family without fitting in time for yourself, you lose your center. Prioritizing the activities that you love will keep you healthy, functioning, and joyful. Doing so is not selfish; it's essential.

So, what is it that keeps your wheel turning? What do you need to do for you? When things feel hectic and chaotic, it might seem harder to fit those activities in, but that's when it's most important. Cherish your core activities and stay grounded.

COURTNEY COMMENT

My dad asked me what my linchpin is as we sat down to write this chapter. Sadly, I couldn't answer. Can you? What did you love doing when you were younger? Do you still do those things today? It's as though becoming an independent adult means giving up what we love. I mean, who has time for hobbies anyway?

Well, we need to make time for them!

In high school and college, I was involved in volleyball, band, mentoring, tutoring, and service. After college, I stopped doing all of these things. It took me years to find my way back to myself outside of work, but I did. I let my hobbies evolve with age. Now, I am my best self when I have a regular yoga and meditation practice, read daily, walk, and spend device-free time doing something creative. I also love discovering a new hole-in-the-wall coffee shop, ordering a fancy brew, and people watching (have any good local spots to recommend?).

Why is it so difficult to find the time and energy to do what is healthiest for us? I find plenty of time to binge watch TV and scroll through Instagram! I believe it comes down to energy. We are exhausted from life's rat race. It's a vicious cycle: you need energy to invest in your linchpin, yet it's your linchpin that gives you energy.

The solution? Try your best. Work to form habits that prioritize your wellbeing. Jump off the hamster wheel for just thirty minutes a day. You'll be better for it. If it's permission you need, I'm giving it to you. And if the snarky voice in your head is saying, "Who made Courtney queen and gave her that authority?!" then you probably need your linchpin now more than ever!

If reading this book *is* your personal investment, then you are one step ahead. You go Glen Coco!

9

Keep a Journal

Your life matters.

I encourage you to keep a journal to record your thoughts, ideas, passions, and memories.

My father passed away before my children were born. I attempted to keep his legacy alive and taught them about their Irish heritage through bedtime stories featuring Clancy the leprechaun, their grandfather's farm, and his immigration to the states. When Courtney was ten years old, she outgrew the leprechaun stories but was fascinated with my father. I think it's because she knew how much he meant to me. One night, after tucking her in, she called me back to her bed. Quietly, she asked, "Do you think Grandpa Owen would have liked me?"

My heart sank. He would have been wrapped around her little finger. I wish he could have told her that himself. For days, her whispered late-night question bounced around in my head. Would my grandchildren know that I love them when I'm no longer here?

That's when I decided to keep a journal. Although I have terrible handwriting and can't spell for the life of me, I have a lot to say and want my family to remember it all when I'm gone. I've been writing in one for the past twenty years.

A journal should be personal and reflect who you are, but beyond that, it can be whatever you want it to be. For me, it is the place where I document every major event, such as birthdays, passings, anniversaries, family trips, and major life accomplishments. The journal is filled with notes, pictures, and mementos (playbills, report cards, personal letters) that help me recapture the feelings of those moments.

**"A life worth living
is a life worth recording."**

—JIM ROHN

I suggest you buy a journal that has space for every day of the year. This will push you to write often. Many days are uneventful—you can simply write three things for which you're grateful. If a daily entry seems too overwhelming, you could start with an undated journal and set a goal to write in it once a week. Or, if you prefer, keep a private digital blog.

My grandson Dylan recently celebrated his eighth birthday, and I decided to share the journal entry from the day he was born. Even though he poked fun at my handwriting and how difficult it was to read, I could tell it meant something to him, and I know it will mean even more as he gets older.

Jim Rohn said it best: "A life worth living is a life worth recording." Your life is worth it. Even if the journal is seen by your eyes only, reflecting on moments in your life will help you understand their importance. And if you choose to share your words, no one will have to guess about the person you were once you're gone; your thinking, personality, and love will jump off the page. Documenting your life is a tribute to your story, and you deserve that honor.

Journal Entries from My Grandson's Birth

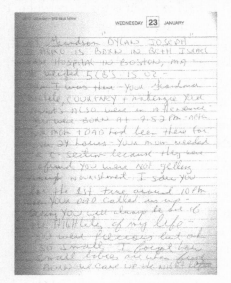

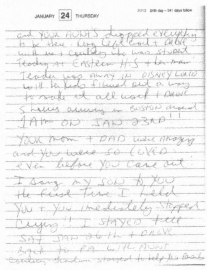

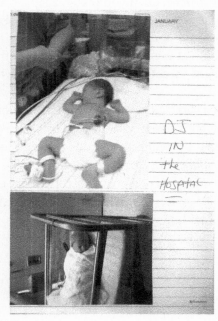

COURTNEY COMMENT

What a gift my dad is giving us with these journals! I am eternally grateful. I also don't know anyone else who journals like he does, so I am here with some options to document your life in a twenty-first century way (bonus: if your handwriting is as bad as my dad's, it won't matter!):

- Use the **1SE** app and record one second of video each day
- Be real on social media—record the good and the bad
- Create a private blog
- Try bullet journaling
- Use an app such as **Qeepsake** (you can actually send a text with pictures and words each day that get added as journal entries on your account)

These are the methods I use, and I find them quick and easy!

10

Be a Tigger

A glass sits on a table and is filled halfway. Those who view the glass as half-full appreciate the water they have. Those who see the glass as half-empty focus on the water that's missing.

This analogy illustrates how the lens through which you view the world alters your perception. Seeing the world positively makes you a happier and more grateful person for the same reasons your thoughts influence your reality. You want to spend your time with "half-full" people and bask in their uplifting energy, while you find yourself exhausted by the "half-empty" people who complain and focus on the negative. These are, to make a *Winnie the Pooh* reference, the Tiggers and Eeyores of the world.

Tiggers don't just see the glass as half-full—they see it as overflowing. Their enthusiasm and positivity are contagious. Eeyores have always been on the other end of the spectrum and find their own personal rain cloud on a beautiful day. They make the simplest tasks unenjoyable. When you spend too much time with Eeyores, you either find yourself oversharing from your glass in a desperate attempt to uplift them, or you begin to view your own glass as lacking.

Of course, the Tigger and Eeyore analogy is a bit simplistic because personality impacts attitude. Tigger is positive, but also naturally social and uplifting. It seems easier for him to look at the world as beautiful.

Eeyore, on the other hand, makes us question whether negativity is a choice. Is he simply grouchy or could he be depressed? Does he need professional help or just some venting and encouragement?

Nothing changed but my gratitude and attitude, yet that changed everything.

Cultivating positivity in your life is not as simple as bouncing around on your tail and smiling at the neighbors. It is difficult, especially for Eeyores. But trying to be positive is beneficial; it increases cardiovascular health and your lifespan, and it lowers levels of stress and depression.

To cultivate a half-full attitude, I challenge you to do the following:

1. Practice Daily Gratitude

Find at least three things to be grateful for each day such as a phone call, a smile from a stranger, or a song on the radio. Gratitude and optimism go hand-in-hand.

During the initial COVID-19 quarantine, I became extremely negative. I am an extroverted person and love eating out and meeting with friends. Like many couples, my wife and I argued over our personal interpretations of lockdown. Michele was extremely cautious and did not want to leave the house, while I wanted to let more people into our social bubble. I told anyone who would listen that my wife had me on house arrest, an unfair comment resulting from my negativity. All I could see was what COVID had taken from me, a half-empty glass. Luckily, I have a wife that reminded me of my privilege—regular visits with my children and grandchildren, financial security, health and safety for my family, and a beautiful home. As soon as I focused on what COVID gave me instead of what it took away, I began to look at the quarantine differently and appreciate the found time. Nothing changed but my gratitude and attitude, yet that changed everything.

2. Accept the Unexpected

Unexpected things happen every day, and all you can control is your reaction to them. Embracing the unexpected will help you turn challenges into triumphs.

Recently, my wife and I arrived at the airport for a returning flight from Mexico to be informed that our flight had been cancelled and we would be spending the night at the gate. Our first reaction was frustration and annoyance. However, we made a conscious decision to make the best of the situation. We had to be there, so why not enjoy it? We made friends with other passengers and laughed the night away. We could have spent the time fuming, but intentionally embracing the situation and having fun instead gave us an everlasting memory. It's not easy to accept that your plans are thwarted, but negativity won't change the outcome, only your perspective can.

3. Work at It Every Day

Being upset is a normal human emotion, but the more you catch yourself responding negatively, the better you become at reacting positively to setbacks. Positivity takes practice, and you should try and cultivate it each day.

Research in positive psychology proves that frequent gratitude leads to better physical health, higher degrees of happiness and optimism, and stronger personal connections. A simple gratitude practice such as writing thank you notes or journaling about what makes you happy results in higher quality sleep, fewer doctor visits, and more fulfilling relationships; and it even incites good deeds in those around you.[4] Put in the work and enjoy the rewards!

Manage your inner Tigger and Eeyore carefully, and you will find more joy and freedom in life.

---

[4] Robert Emmons, "Why Gratitude Is Good," *Greater Good Magazine*, November 16, 2010, https://greatergood.berkeley.edu/article/item/why_gratitude_is_good. Last accessed July 28, 2021.

COURTNEY COMMENT

My dad can be obnoxiously positive. One of his common "Geneisms" is, "It's all part of the journey!" and this is often exclaimed as you're crying over a missed promotion or trying to forget an embarrassing moment.

I acknowledge that you might be sitting there thinking, *This is what I paid for? Another "be happy" speech making me feel guilty about my feelings?*

Our generation has a habit of presenting the photoshopped version of our lives on social media while flaunting shirts that say, "NO BAD DAYS." I am here to reassure you that our advice is not that. My dad has his bad days too. Just yesterday he caught himself in the middle of yet another rant about my mom ordering one too many Amazon packages, even though they already agreed he'd let the discussion go. Just as Tigger and Eeyore become close friends, understanding each other's flaws and balancing each other out, you too are entitled to your good and bad moments.

But when you do remember to look at the bright side of a bad situation, it benefits you. So simply try, and that's enough. This advice is here to remind you of the power of positivity, not perfection. Sometimes we do the right things and feel great. And sometimes we just need to complain about the Amazon package. There is no judgment here! I just hope your good days outweigh your bad ones. And if you ever find yourself searching for a missing tail to make you feel whole, I hope you'll be able to call forth that positive energy to bounce your way through.

11

Be Present

Living in the moment has become a mantra for the masses, but it's easier said than done. How can you embrace this approach to living? Eliminate distraction!

In my opinion, smartphones are the biggest hindrance to being present. Notifications constantly announce social media updates. Our calendar reminds us what's up next. Calls and texts connect us to people anywhere but here. Apps entice us with news updates, addictive games, and emails from work. This tiny device has a big presence.

Just how much attention do we give our phones? More than we consciously know! A study of approximately eight hundred participants tested how the placement and status of each participant's phone affected their cognitive functioning.[5] Cognitive tasks were completed with either the phone turned over on the table, placed in a bag or pocket, or left in another room. Each scenario presented tasks with the phones turned on and then powered off. The finding? The mere presence of your phone affects cognitive function, even when you are resisting looking

---

[5] Adrian F. Ward, Kristen Duke, Ayelet Gneezy, and Maarten W. Bos, "Brain Drain: The Mere Presence of One's Own Smartphone Reduces Available Cognitive Capacity," *Journal of the Association for Consumer Research* 2 no. 2 (April 2, 2018): https://www.journals.uchicago.edu/doi/10.1086/691462. Last accessed July 28, 2021.

at it and notifications are silenced. The closer the phone, the bigger the negative impact on performance. Even with a phone turned off, cognitive capacity suffers.

I conducted my own social experiment to see if getting rid of phones could help my dinner guests and me be more present. I coached my son's AAU basketball team, and like most teenage boys, my players were glued to their phones between games. When we sat down to dinner at a restaurant, every player was attached to his phone. So, I told them they could put their phones away or pay for their own meals.

Of course, the boys reluctantly placed their devices in their pockets. What happened next? We connected! It was one of the greatest meals we had with the group, and dinner lasted twice as long. I learned my players' fears of college rejection, laughed along as they shared dating tips, and even convinced one of them to try calamari. With the phones out, we never would have had these conversations, the connection, or the experience. Ironically, the very device we hope will connect us to others far and wide disengages us from those right in front of us.

Ironically, the very device we hope will connect us to others far and wide disengages us from those right in front of us.

I challenge you to leave your phone in the car or another room the next time you have a meal. Observe how you feel. Are you stressed? Are you distracted? Are you relieved? Focus on the food and the company. If this is difficult, it might be a sign of how disconnected you've become. If the thought of doing this seems impossible, you might have some work to do. But who doesn't?

COURTNEY COMMENT

As a high school English teacher, I see the impact of cell phones on attention and engagement every second of every day. If you ask a teen to put their phone away, it's as if you are asking them to cut off a limb. In fact, I've had long conversations with my students who claim they would rather cut off a limb than surrender their phones (teens can be very dramatic!).

I share the research on how phones negatively impact their work in class, engagement in discussion, and general cognition. They logically understand, but they cannot bring themselves to ditch the device.

So, I took the plunge. I made a classroom policy to drop phones in individual cubbies on their way into class. After days of grunts, a habit formed. And as the habit formed, there was space for new experiences, new focus, new engagement, and new learning. Three months into the experiment, I gave my students the choice whether or not to continue the cell phone policy. Although I did not get 100% of the vote in favor, I had a majority support in each class. So we continued this mindfulness practice.

Sometimes the hardest actions are the ones we need the most. If a highly social sixteen-year-old can do it, you can too! So, join in and make airplane mode the norm so we can all start living in the moment.

12

Never Underestimate the Power of Humor

Humor is one of life's greatest medicines. Nothing brings people together like a good laugh! I grew up in a house where my father never wasted the chance to tell a joke, and I learned at a young age that laughter strengthens relationships. When you share a belly laugh with someone, you're bonded. I grew up loving practical jokes and prank phone calls, which my oldest friends still endure today.

Nothing brings people together like a good laugh!

Humor can be used to break the ice in many situations, especially ones that appear formal and cold. Let your humor be the catalyst to warm things up. That's exactly what was needed at a weekend-long Catholic pre-marital retreat called Pre-Cana that my wife and I attended. I'm Catholic and Michele is Jewish, so of course she was nervous and did not know what to expect.

Each of the twenty-two couples at the retreat was tasked with introducing themselves by telling the story of how they met. Couple after couple told romantic stories of looking deep into each other's eyes and *just knowing*. Finally, it was our turn. I began to tell our "story": "My fiancé used to work at an X-rated movie theater, and there was just something about the way she buttered the popcorn…" Michele jumped up, frantically correcting, "He's lying! I'm a speech pathologist!" And everyone was rolling, including the priest. Michele, although embarrassed, breathed easier. I admit, I pushed the envelope a bit with this one, but we immediately went from a room of almost fifty strangers to a feeling of community amongst friends.

In tense situations, my biggest role model, Abraham Lincoln, was also known to take a break to tell a joke in hopes of relaxing the group. For example, during the Civil War, Lincoln's cabinet was reaching an impasse on battle strategy, so he stopped the meeting to tell them about Ethan Allen, a controversial and somewhat comical American figure known to be brash. The story goes that at a dinner in England with many powerful figures, the British poked fun at the visiting American by putting a large picture of George Washington in the outhouse. When he returned from the bathroom, they asked what he thought of the décor. Lincoln loved to share Allen's response: "There is nothing to make an Englishman shit quicker than the sight of General George Washington."[6] And the mood became lighter. They were then able to calmly reengage in discussion.

Everyone should have a few jokes they can tell when the moment is appropriate. Not sure how to cultivate humor? Steal some material—I get a joke of the day in my inbox each morning. The gift of laughter is one of the best you can give, no matter where you got it.[7]

---

[6] Joshua Trudell, "9 Times a U.S. President Used Profane Language in Office," *Rare*, February 15, 2019, https://rare.us/rare-life/9-times-a-president-used-profanity/. Last accessed July 28, 2021.

[7] Brandon M. Savage, Heid L. Lujan, Raghavendar R. Thipparthi, and Stephen E. DiCarlo, "Humor, laughter, learning, and health! A brief review," *Advances in Physiology Education*, 41, no. 3 (July 5, 2017): 341-347, https://journals.physiology.org/doi/full/10.1152/advan.00030.2017?rss=1&. Last accessed July 28, 2021.

COURTNEY COMMENT

As a teacher, I love watching the impact of humor on community and learning.

I pride myself on my teacher-student relationships and classroom community. I give a lot of the credit to humor. I let teens be teens and never take myself too seriously. When I was student teaching, we kept a bulletin board of all the funny antics and quotations in our classes, and students loved it. They were so excited to make additions. Some of those students stay in touch to this day because of the community we formed.

When entertained and laughing, students also learn better. As a result, good teaching is performative. I will never forget the difference between vertical and horizontal because my fifth-grade teacher dove on the ground, sprawled out flat, and said, "Hey, now I'm horizontal!" The students applauded and laughed hysterically.

Humor helps cements learning, too. Whenever we laugh about a topic, students are more likely to remember it when evaluated. One literary term I teach is "scapegoat," a person who is blamed for others' wrongdoings. One year, a student referred to a character as a "*space-goat*," and we all, including her, laughed until we couldn't breathe. We proceeded to draw the character in a spacesuit with all of those who ostracized her in the peripheral. We made the connection that scape-goats feel like aliens and are pushed to the outside, so the mistake made sense! That year, not one student in the class forgot what a scapegoat was come exam time.

Humor feels good, but it also works! More humorous content increases alertness and attention span, reduces stress, increases creativity, aids memory, helps with self-esteem, and even increases motivation. It's no wonder humor improves student performance!

Next time you need to study or keep someone's attention, go for the laugh!

13

There's No Harm in Asking

Whether it's relationships, business, or pleasure, there will be times when you assume there is no way to get what you want. There will be times when "no" is the only response you can imagine. And if you never ask for what it is that you want, you'll always prove yourself right.

**If you accept assumptions as truth,
you might miss out on something amazing.**

But what if your assumption is wrong? We often accept beliefs as truth without ever asking for what it is that we want. No one at your workplace has ever been promoted in fewer than three years, so why think you're any different? Your friends complain that the newest restaurant is booked out for two months, so why try to get a reservation?

Why? Because you just don't know! That early promotion might be within reach. A reservation could have opened up last minute. Or maybe it didn't. But if you don't ask, you have no chance at being pleasantly surprised.

By simply asking, I was able to make some dreams come true for my family. Every four years, my family and friends get together to attend the

Jets versus Eagles NFL game. We're a group divided and love the tradition of bringing the feuding football fans together. When I spoke with the salesperson to purchase the tickets, I decided to ask for the impossible: a chance to meet some of the players. Although I couldn't get a meet-and-greet, I *was* able to score pre-game sideline passes and the opportunity for two members of my family to help carry the flag on the field before kickoff. By simply asking, I secured some incredible experiences, and my brother says carrying the flag was one of the highlights of his life. Even though we didn't get a "yes," we were pleasantly surprised by what we did get. Of course, not every "no" story turns out as happily as this one, but it's still worth trying.

And then there is that rare time I get the "yes," plain and simple, and even I'm shocked. My famous "yes" resulted in what my kids refer to as the miracle trip. Each year, RCI sends its staff members who exceed their annual goals on a weeklong vacation. One year, my company's trip to Mexico was preceded by a terrible snowstorm in Philadelphia. Somehow, the flight wasn't cancelled, but as we drove to the airport, we were the only car on the road and heaps of snow lined the shoulder. We arrived at the gate to a plane with no crew because the snow delayed them too. The airport felt empty, and the plane clearly wasn't taking off any time soon. Most of my employees left and returned home.

Since the flight still hadn't been cancelled, my family and a few others decided to wait it out and hope we'd take off eventually. My college-aged kids were all together for the first time in months, and I desperately wanted to make the trip happen for them. My business partner and I decided to walk around and check for any departing flights. Miraculously, we found a chartered plane leaving for Cancun within the hour. It couldn't hurt to ask if they had any open seats, right? It just so happened that many of their passengers were snowed in. Somehow, I was able to get my remaining staff and family on this charter, the only flight leaving the airport all morning. As the plane took off, we were astonished. All I had to do was ask!

When you do ask for the seemingly impossible, be ready for any answer. I once told a car salesman that if he could give me the car on display for $15,000 less than the sticker price, I'd walk away with it right then and there. His response? "Sold!" Unfortunately, even with a $15,000 discount, the car was still too expensive. I walked away feeling embarrassed, and of course with no car. When you ask, be ready to act!

Life surprises you. People surprise you. If you accept assumptions as truth, you might miss out on something amazing.

COURTNEY COMMENT

My dad has given my siblings and me the most amazing memories by simply asking. My oldest sister was obsessed with Hanson in her teens. When they were scheduled to come to the local radio station, my dad decided to call them up and ask if we could visit and meet the band. Next thing you know, we're sitting in the studio taking pictures with Isaac, Taylor, and Zach!

One of my other favorite memories is when my dad was able to get my sisters and me on a Nickelodeon commercial. This was my fifteen minutes of fame! He saw people filming while we were visiting Nickelodeon Studios and asked if his daughters could be in the commercial. Their response? "Sure!" Fast-forward a few months and my kindergarten friends were freaking out over my face on their TV (for a whole 0.5 seconds).

Thanks, Dad, for always asking!

Me? I find it incredibly difficult to ask for such unusual requests, worried I will be told "no" and seen as an annoyance. I can attest that the more you do it, the more the confidence builds, and the easier it gets. I still find it hard to work up the nerve sometimes, but just last month I was able to secure a discount on daycare just by asking—and that's worth a little discomfort to me!

14

Use Open-Ended Questions to Build Connections

The best way to get to know someone is to ask the right questions. Open-ended questions help you understand what matters most to a person and who they are at their core. I often ask questions over a meal to help break the ice and forge a deeper connection with the people in my life. Employees, coworkers, friends, and family alike have all been on the receiving end of my seemingly random queries.

Develop relationships faster and more meaningfully.

On a recent vacation with my son and his future in-laws, I asked many questions to get to know them better. One night, I asked, "What's one thing you love about yourself?" Rob, my son's future father-in-law, explained that he was consistent and could be counted on. I knew this to be true from how he raised his girls and grew his career. Recognizing that my son would now have this man in his family made me feel grateful—I grew a profound respect for Rob.

What I did not expect was my future daughter-in-law's struggle to answer this question. What did we do? We wrapped her in love and helped her see herself though our eyes by highlighting her incredible qualities: her work ethic, commitment to family, and love for children to name a few. She felt wonderful, and we felt appreciative to have had the opportunity to share these sentiments.

I encourage you to have questions in mind when you go to a meeting or meal and observe how asking them allows you to develop relationships faster and more meaningfully. Be ready to share your responses too (have a discussion, not an interrogation).

Example Questions

- If you could choose to sit next to anyone at dinner you haven't met before, who would it be and why?
- What's the best advice you have ever received?
- What's your most cherished childhood memory?
- What advice would you give your fifteen-year-old self?
- Who was your favorite teacher or coach and why?
- If you could change one thing in the world today, what would it be?
- What is something you do that makes you lose track of time?
- Who is your favorite relative and why?
- What has been your greatest struggle and what have you learned from it?

You never know how the questions will help you get to know one another better and deepen bonds. Take the opportunity to truly understand the people in your life. You will never regret taking the time to strengthen these connections.

COURTNEY COMMENT

Imagine bringing a boyfriend home to meet your dad with these questions up his sleeve! Some daughters would roll their eyes, but I loved seeing who could open up when asked a profound question and handle being in the hot seat.

Just remember to read the room when asking open-ended questions. My dad is very socially and emotionally intelligent and can instantly read nuanced details in a group setting. He inherently knows what types of questions are best to ask, when to ask them, how many to ask, and to whom. He effortlessly uses people's answers to bridge to new topics and share his own related stories. This is not so easy for everyone.

Think about the group before a get-together or meal and gather a few questions that might be relevant. Consider your answers. And if the timing feels right, ask one or two. Let it flow naturally. When you do it right, these questions spark great conversation.

PART TWO

JOB SEARCH

15

Understanding
the Role of the Resume

L ooking for a job? At any point in your life if the answer to this question is "yes," you will need a resume on hand. I have received and
reviewed thousands of resumes and have noticed that it is both an art
and a science to organize your professional qualifications and experience. Your resume should be as aesthetically pleasing as it is informative.

**The resume has one essential purpose:
secure the interview!**

The resume has one essential purpose: secure the interview! What is
the best way to do this? See below.

Resume Sections in Order

- Name and contact information
- Summary or objective
- Professional history
- Educational history
- Skills and abilities

Resume Dos

- *Personalize Your Objective:* Customize your objective to the job.
- *Tailor Key Achievements:* Under relevant work experience, include specific work accomplishments that relate to the job (and quantify them whenever possible).
- *Prioritize Relevant Skills:* Put your most applicable skills first and change the order depending upon the job.
- *Acknowledge Red Flags:* If a portion of your resume could discount you, explain (e.g., if you spent less than two years with a company, briefly state in one phrase why the move was made).
- *Customize Your Cover Letter:* Highlight your biggest accomplishments and make a personal connection to show you're a strong fit for the role (use the specific company name).
- *Use Powerful Verbs:* Use vivid verbs to start each bulleted phrase (avoid the verb "work"—everyone works).
- *Edit:* Avoid typos and errors.
- *Adopt an Approachable Format:* Use bullet points and organization to make your resume easy and quick to read; utilize format features to emphasize the most important points.
- *Plan for Next Steps:* Prepare your references so that you can contact them if your interview process moves quickly.

Resume Don'ts

- Don't use more than one page.
- Don't ramble (avoid wordiness).
- Don't be too general.
- Don't include irrelevant experience or personal information like hobbies.
- Don't include a picture.
- Don't use an unprofessional or extravagant format in order to stand out (simple and approachable is good).
- Don't stray from chronological order when listing experience—start with your most recent jobs and work backward.
- Don't emphasize older jobs over recent ones.
- Don't list references.
- Don't use a font size smaller than ten.

- Don't save or share in an editable format (use a pdf with your surname in the file name).
- Don't list your high school.
- Don't lie.

Read that last one again. Lying might feel harmless and be tempting because it could help you get ahead, but I promise you that the truth comes out through background checks and information verification. One executive I worked with said he had a degree from a certain college. Although he had the diploma, 153 credits, and attended graduation, one of his last classes was pass/fail, and he failed because he never wrote the final paper. He was never awarded his degree, which lost him a role twenty years later. I had another executive who said he worked at a previous company for twenty-five years. He was offered a job and was even given $15,000 to relocate, but when his information was verified, the company uncovered that he hadn't been at the previous company for the last three of the twenty-five years, and they rescinded the offer (and took back the $15,000). Resist the urge to be dishonest on your resume!

I highly recommend that you keep your resume updated. Often the best opportunities present themselves when you're not looking. It's also easy to forget accomplishments over time, so update your resume as you acquire new skills and recognitions to have the relevant information on hand when needed.

The more you tailor your resume to a specific job description, the more likely you are to get invited in for an interview. You should address the company and job in your cover letter, but also revise your objective, experience, and skills with each new opportunity to highlight the specific job qualifications. I have seen many people miss opportunities because their resumes were too broad.

Before submitting a resume, have friends and trusted mentors review it and share their feedback. Use their input to revise your document. Your resume is your first impression, so eliminate all mistakes. There are companies you can hire to help with your resume, but a quick web search brings up endless templates and examples to peruse. If you utilize all your resources, you will create a resume that will get your foot in the door!

COURTNEY COMMENT

Do you think I can put "Instagram sleuth" under skills and abilities? I mean, it is a transferrable skill....

In all seriousness, think outside the box for the skills section of your resume. Only list skills that match the job description. You would be surprised by how many pertinent skills you have that will help you excel in the workplace though you may not have prior work experience. Skills can come from your studies, volunteer work, clubs, interests, and trainings. For example, have you used Microsoft Word, Excel, PowerPoint, and OneNote throughout your education? You might be able to list Microsoft Office proficiency as a skill.

There are two types of skills employers look for:

1. **Soft Skills:** Skills that are more subjective and interpersonal. They are universal.
   Examples: problem solving, adaptability, collaboration, and leadership.

2. **Hard Skills:** Skills that are quantifiable and teachable. They are usually specific to a job.
   Examples: languages, data presentation, typing speed, data analysis, research, and writing.

Take some time to think about skills you have acquired and how they transfer to the jobs you are pursuing. But remember, only list skills you truly have and always include the ones that match the job description best. You want to include five to ten skills on your resume and have a good mix of both soft and hard skills.

16

How to Increase Your Number of Interviews

Interviewing is a numbers game—the more resumes you submit, the more interviews you'll get, and the more interviews you get, the more opportunities you'll have. My goal is to help you get several interviews so that you can put yourself in the best position to find the right role for you.

The more interviews you go on, the more practice you get at interviewing, and the clearer it becomes what your next career move should be. I placed an executive who was sure he wanted to work for a Fortune 2,000 firm, but I suggested that he keep an open mind and explore various options. He received multiple job offers, but ultimately accepted one with a small boutique firm instead of one with the top company in his industry because of the people and the role. Through the interviewing process, he realized he preferred to be a big fish in a small pond. It is this type of introspection and personal learning that comes from exploring opportunities and interviewing with various companies.

Interviewing is a numbers game.

How to Increase Your Number of Interviews

1. Work Your Network

The best way to secure interviews is to network. Sending your resume along to the right person might be the very connection you need to bring your resume to the top of the pile. Use your college career center to connect with alumni in your field or ask your college professors if they have any contacts. Family connections are also great opportunities to network. Share what you are looking for with your contact and see if they know anyone to pass your resume along to.

2. Post Everywhere

Again, the more places you make your resume available, the more chances to be invited to interview. I recommend that you post your resume on LinkedIn, Indeed, CareerBuilder, Monster, ZipRecruiter, Glassdoor, and USAJobs. Also be sure to research job boards in your region or ones specific to your profession and post there.

3. Search Daily

Check for new job postings at least once a day. Look on company websites and job boards. Dedicate a specific time of the day to search for jobs and ensure you stay well-informed.

4. Connect with Recruiters

Recruiters can submit your resume for job prospects and help secure interviews. I suggest you reach out to recruiting firms that specialize in your field since they'll have the most prospects and alert you of opportunities you might not otherwise know about. To find recruiters in your industry, try these sites:

- https://www.recruiterly.com/
- https://www.onlinerecruitersdirectory.com/
- https://www.i-recruit.com/
- http://www.searchfirm.com/

The next chapter will walk you through working with a recruiter.

5. Use Strategic Targeting

Target specific companies that hire people with your type of background. Reach out to those companies through a department leader. Chapter Eighteen goes into detail about how to do this.

6. Keep an Open Mind

It's never a bad idea to expand your search parameters. Again, interviewing is a numbers game, so keep an open mind. You don't have to take a job offer, but you want to be the one in the position to accept or decline it. Plus, job offers can surprise you!

If you use these tips to help you secure interviews, you'll be in a great place to learn about yourself professionally and find the best opportunities.

COURTNEY COMMENT

One of the best ways to network is through Greek life organizations. At Lehigh, Greek life was king. I felt I could reach out to any member of my sorority, regardless of where they lived or attended college, and then have an instant connection. I know of so many people who received their interviews and first jobs through Greek life connections.

My husband Rich is a member of the Knights of Columbus, and his father attended meetings with an accountant at Deloitte. Rich used this connection and landed his first job out of college! Always look for those relationships and then pay it forward when you have the chance to help someone else.

Not a member of a sorority or fraternity? You can network using your school's alumni organization, family friends, clubs, former teachers, internship connections, community leaders, and more. Work any and all connections!

17

Working with a Recruiter

Recruiters play an important role in your job search, especially as you advance in your career (and I'm not just saying this because I am one). Recruiters are a great tool to help you get the role of your dreams.

Your first job out of school will most likely come from an internship, connection, or college recruiter. I always recommend attending campus job fairs and networking. After your first job, there is a large world of recruiting that opens up to you, including different types of firms and specialists in your industry.

One way to work with a recruiter is to reach out. Try one of these methods:

- Ask colleagues in your field for recruiter references
- Research the specialist firms in your field

In many cases, you won't need to seek them out. In most professions, the more experience you have, the more likely it is that a recruiter will find you and share opportunities. Whether you reach out to them, or they contact you, it's important to know the right questions to ask a recruiter and how to build a lasting relationship that will benefit your career.

First, identify the type of recruiter and firm you're working with to assure it's the right match for you. There are four major types:

1. In-House Recruiter

An in-house recruiter works for the company that is searching for a new hire. Large companies will often have their own recruiters on staff to fill their frequent hiring needs. An in-house recruiter's only client is their company. They fill multiple positions at once, so if a particular role isn't right for you, they can sometimes shift you to another role at the company. When you submit a resume to a company, like many people do to find their first jobs, an in-house recruiter is often the one who will follow up. If you are contacted by an in-house recruiter, it is helpful to ask if they are contracted or a permanent employee. A full-time in-house recruiter will have more insight, guidance, and information about the hiring authority.

2. Temporary Staffing Firms

Temporary staffing firms help you find short-term positions quickly. This type of firm is beneficial if you're currently unemployed or employed in another temporary position and will be on the hunt for work again soon. The interviewing process moves quickly. The staffing firm pays your salary (minus their fee), and the company pays them. Companies like hiring through temporary staffing firms for many reasons:

- It lets them have a trial run with an employee before committing
- They don't pay your benefits (the staffing company does)
- You're paid only if you work (no vacation or sick time)
- It helps fill temporary needs, such as a short-term project
- They can fire you immediately with no repercussions

Yes, there is less job security and stability with temp positions, but there are benefits too. If you prove yourself, you could be hired permanently. You're also given an opportunity to get to know the work culture before committing to them long-term.

3. Contingency Recruiting Firms

In some ways, the recruiting industry is like the medical field. Like a general practitioner, a contingency recruiter comprises most of the field and is a good starting point in a job search. They have general knowledge and primarily fill starting to mid-level positions. Understand that when you work with a contingency recruiter, multiple recruiters and even the company itself are trying to fill the same role. One recruiter probably has little control over the hiring process and might be unable to give you interview feedback quickly. Contingency recruiters work hard to get as many candidates as they can to interview because they only get paid if their candidate is hired. When working with this type of recruiter, ask if they're working with someone in HR, talent acquisition, or the hiring manager. If they're working directly with talent acquisition (an internal recruiter) or the hiring manager, their ability to get you feedback is much greater.

4. Retained Search Firms

There are also retained search firms. RCI is one of these companies. They normally fill more senior level positions, and they work exclusively with the client. The retained firm either fills the role or no one does. A retained search firm manages the entire search process, and even internal referrals are vetted through them. The firm gets paid whether the role is filled or not. Retained search firms are experts and specialists in their field, and they know all the talent in the industry. This type of recruiter can be extremely valuable in your career because they know the best opportunities. When forming a relationship with a retained recruiter, tell them what you like best about your current role, what you like least, and how you see your career progressing. This way, if a unique opportunity arises, you'll be kept in the know.

**You have nothing to lose
by keeping an open mind.**

No matter the type of firm, my best piece of advice is to always return the call when contacted by a recruiter. You have nothing to lose by keeping an open mind about positions. Even if you're currently content, call back with the goal of building a relationship with the recruiter. Before making the call, research the firm. When on the phone, make a connection and be helpful (if you know someone who would want to hear about the role being presented, pass on the referral). When you do need a new job down the line, you will then have contacts.

My brother-in-law Jesse was satisfied at his job for twenty years and never returned recruiting calls. Then his company was sold, and the resulting changes made him more open to opportunities. He returned a recruiter's call for the first time in years and interviewed with a Fortune 500 company closer to home. After the series of interviews, he left excited and was hoping for an offer. Then there was silence! He kept reaching out for feedback, but the recruiter never returned his calls (shame on them). There is no excuse for the recruiter's actions. However, if my brother-in-law had a previous relationship with this recruiter, he more than likely would have received a call back. The company probably moved on to a different candidate, and it is extremely unprofessional of the recruiter to not relay this information. You might be able to avoid a similar scenario if you make the effort to return recruiter calls and make connections. Then, when you do need their help to advance your career, you will be guided through your job search by a recruiter that is an invested partner rather than a fleeting stranger.

When you return that first recruiter call, here are some key questions to ask:

- What field do you specialize in?
- Are you a retained search firm working exclusively with the client?
- Have you made any placements with this firm before? (If yes, this is a real positive!)
- Who are you dealing with, HR or the hiring manager?
- If they are not retained, ask: Do you know how many firms your client is working with to fill this position?
- Have you presented any previous candidates for this role? What was the feedback?
- How many other candidates will you be presenting?
- What are my strengths and weaknesses in comparison to other candidates?
- Why do you feel I'm a good candidate?
- Can we schedule time to prepare for the interview?
- How long will it take for you to get feedback on the interview?
- Can we schedule a call to debrief after the interview?
- If the interview goes well, what is the next step?
- Can you share the salary range?

Build these professional relationships and understand exactly the type of firm you're working with. If you have a strong recruiter, they might place you multiple times in your career. Regardless of your plans, there is no harm in having a conversation!

COURTNEY COMMENT

I don't know any teachers who use recruiters, but I have seen the magic of recruiting through my husband.

When my husband took his first role after Deloitte, he used a contingency recruiter who was referred by a respected colleague and specializes in accounting in his region. She sent him on many interviews and found him a role that helped him grow professionally. When he moved to a new area to be with me (can you blame him?!), his trusted recruiter was no longer the best resource because he was in a different state. Luckily, she had coworkers in our region for him to work with.

Later in his career, he built a relationship with a recruiter who understood his skills and needs. This recruiter sent Rich on interviews at two crucial times, and Rich received job offers to advance his career in both scenarios. This relationship was so strong that the recruiter actually helped Rich fill a role at one of his companies.

Fast-forward to today, and Rich is thriving and happy in his current role. He found this one by submitting a resume and working with an in-house recruiter. The role he interviewed for was filled by someone else, but they liked Rich so much they created a new position at the company for him that would highlight his strengths—a huge advantage of working with a full-time in-house recruiter at a business you respect.

Thank you, recruiters, for helping my husband support our family and grow in his craft time and time again!

18

Dressing for Success

You don't get a second chance at a first impression. On an interview, the first impression starts with your appearance. To the interviewer, the way you carry yourself shows how you will represent the company.

You can never go wrong by over-dressing. When in doubt, wear a suit. You'll never be judged as too formal, but you might be judged if you're too casual.

You can never go wrong by overdressing.

When my son-in-law Doug was in high school, he sought a job at the local supermarket. Every teenager in town wanted to work there because of the pay and the flexible hours. Doug wore a tie to the interview, and the manager hired him on the spot, largely because he was the first person to ever dress up. This showed him that Doug took the opportunity seriously. No job is too casual to interview in a suit!

On the other hand, I have seen people lose jobs over wrinkled shirts, casual shoes, flashy lipstick, and slacks. Judging someone based on appearance might not seem fair, but it is a reality. I have also had clients that were eliminated because of piercings and tattoos. Though I don't personally agree with these decisions, I share them so you know what to expect.

Not sure exactly what to wear? Below is a general overview.

Clothing

- Solid color suit or tailored dress (navy, black, or dark gray is best)
- Long-sleeved collared button-down shirt in white or coordinated neutral color
- No intricate patterns
- Conservative attire
- Fit—not too tight or too loose
- Close-toed, conservative, and coordinated shoes (polished and cleaned)
- Coordinated belt
- Ironed clothes
- Solid, neutral pantyhose
- Tie (for men; avoid busy patterns and bright colors)
- Dark socks

Accessories

- Little or no jewelry
- Portfolio or briefcase (with professional business cards, resumes, and a laptop to share work)

Other

- No cologne, perfume, or aftershave
- Styled, professional hair (avoid too much product)
- Fresh breath
- Silenced phone
- Clean and cut nails
- Natural, understated make-up
- Clean-shaven or well-groomed facial hair

These guidelines are for business formal attire. If a company specifies business casual, you can skip the suit, but do wear professional tops and avoid jeans.

Keep in mind that the company, industry, and location can affect dress code. For example, many startup companies dress very casually. Jeans might be appropriate, but only dress that way if explicitly instructed. In this scenario, the jeans should be tailored and without rips, tears, and distress. Make sure you still look clean and polished.

Participating in a virtual interview? The same rules apply. Wear a suit unless otherwise directed. You must also find an area for your interview with a professional and neutral backdrop that is quiet and has strong Internet connection. A good family friend recently interviewed on Zoom for a job he was very excited about. To his disappointment, he was not selected for the job and later found out it was because he was not wearing a tie.

Whatever you wear, make sure it's appropriate and presentable. If you could offend one person with your outfit, choose something else. Always err on the side of professional and conservative. Your attire should complement you, not be a distraction. Couple this with a firm handshake and a calm, strong voice and your first impression will be a positive one. When you prepare and dress professionally, you will be more confident and crush the interview!

COURTNEY COMMENT

I hate the idea, especially as a woman, that you are judged by your appearance. But, reality is reality. As a female, dressing for the interview is even more confusing because there are more options.

My best advice is to follow in Coco Chanel's footsteps and invest in a power suit! There is too much guesswork that goes into whether a blouse or certain pair of pants is appropriate enough. A plain suit with a collared button-down shirt will never fail. Check out the department stores when they are running sales and then hit up the local tailor so it fits perfectly.

19

Using the Targeted Approach

When you submit a resume, it will often get filed away with hundreds of others, but with the right career connections, you can make it out of that resume pile. How do you make personal connections with leaders in your industry who might be able to give you a foot in the door or the advice needed to do so? It all boils down to relationship building and networking (and no, you don't have to have any previous connections). What I refer to as the targeted approach is simple and will help you do just that. See the process outlined below.

The Targeted Approach

1. Identify the top companies in your industry within a fifty-mile radius of where you're willing to live.

2. Gather contact information for the industry leaders at those companies (your networking "targets"). A leader's title varies depending upon your field. For example, if you're an engineer, you might look for the lead engineer or department head at your target companies. As a teacher, reach out to principals and supervisors. Wanting to break into sales? Reach out to chief sales officers.

3. Send each of your targets a short personal email asking for advice rather than a job (see sample email below). The initial email is not the time to send a resume or ask specific questions. Most senior people, no matter how busy, will take the time to respond to and advise young, passionate professionals looking to start or grow in their field. Many senior people have children or nieces and nephews, and they most likely hope someone would do the same for them.

4. If given the opportunity to talk to an industry leader, share your passion and goals. Ask, and really listen to, the following:

   - How did you get your start?
   - Do you have any advice for me?
   - Are there any positions you're aware of that I should pursue?
   - Is there anyone you think I should talk to that could help me break into the industry?
   - Can I follow up with you and keep you updated on my search and career?

It all boils down to relationship building and networking (and no, you don't have to have any previous connections).

The targeted approach may result in job opportunities, but your primary goal is to make a connection and get guidance to help you develop your career.

I was once contacted by a charity that helps foster children with the college admissions process and connects them with career mentors. They asked if I would help a young man find his first job after graduating from Temple University. His degree? Sports Management! Everyone wants to enter this field, but it's one of the hardest to break into and almost impossible without a personal connection. After a few minutes of talking with this young man, it was clear that he had a real passion for the industry. I agreed to help him if he promised me two things:

1. He was prepared to move to Des Moines, Iowa and work for a Low-A baseball team if he was lucky enough to get that.
2. He would have a plan B.

He told me he was ready to go anywhere, take anything, and try sales if we failed. He was committed, and that's when the targeted approach came in.

He had already submitted his resume to every major-league Philadelphia team from the Flyers to the Eagles. Not surprisingly, he received zero responses. Like those teams, I receive more resumes a week than I can possibly respond to. When will I always respond? When I receive a personal email from a young person who expresses passion for my industry and asks for guidance. This was my mentee's next move: follow the steps for the targeted approach to send the type of email that will get a response.

His first round of emails garnered a reply from the chief marketing officer of the 76ers. In preparation for their call, we practiced asking for specific advice and sharing both his passion for the field and his professional goals. They spoke for an hour, and everything fell into place quickly thereafter. This young man was invited to meet with six people that Friday! I prepped him using the five-step interview process that I share in Chapters Nineteen to Twenty-Three of this book, and he was hired to work in corporate sales for the 76ers. He now works for the LA Kings. His first round of emails is what made it all possible!

The targeted approach can work in any industry. If you reach out to enough people, you will get a response. Your process might not be as quick or prosperous as the young man's in the example above, but it's a numbers game just as with interviewing. If you learn one thing from one conversation, it's worth the effort.

Sample Email for the Targeted Approach

Subject: Young Professional Seeking Advice

Dear Mr./Ms. _____

I am a young professional [or college graduate from _____ with a passion for the _____ industry. After doing research, it is clear that you're a thought leader in the field, and I was hoping you would be willing to spend a few minutes with me to share advice on how to break into [or advance in] the business.

I know your time is valuable, and I promise not to waste it. If given the opportunity in the future, I will pay it forward.

Sincerely,

[Your Name]
[Contact Information]

COURTNEY COMMENT

Having trouble accessing the contact information for your targets?

Search for the formula the company uses to configure their email addresses and apply it to your target professional's name. For example, if you find someone at the same company whose email address is their full name with a specific domain, use that combination to formulate your industry leader's email address too.

If that information is unavailable or you cannot find a name or title, you can try calling the company and asking for contact information that way. The effort will be worth it!

20

Acing the Interview
Step 1: Rapport

In the next five chapters, I will share my five-step interview preparation process that teaches you how to interview. The tips I reveal apply to all interviewing: college internships, your first job, and senior level positions alike. I have trained everyone from my children's teenage friends to fifty-five-year-old CEOs using this method, and it results in success across the board. Interviewed multiple times without getting an offer? Utilize this process and capture the job on the very next try.

Interviewing is a game, and the better you know the rules, the better you'll perform. When you get the opportunity to interview for your dream job, you want to be prepared to play the best game of your life. If you take the time to go on an interview, you should have one goal: get the offer! You can always decline it, but you want to be the one with the power to make that choice. If you practice and follow these five steps, you'll have a much better chance of being in that position.

Never underestimate the power of human connection.

The first goal of any interview is to establish chemistry and rapport with your interviewer. Often, applicants sit down and jump right into the nitty-gritty, but if you can change the pace and make a personal connection first, you'll leave an impression and set yourself apart from other candidates. Think of it this way—if you're the one choosing between two final candidates with the same experience and credentials, how would you decide between the two? The tie breaker usually goes to the person you connected with most. Who doesn't want to surround themselves with people they like?

At RCI, we give our clients (who are the ones doing the hiring) a short list of the top five candidates rated in order based upon how strong a match they are for the position. You would be surprised by how many times clients pick a candidate lower on the list because they are well-liked. We had a global consulting firm with a hiring manager that was known to be an extremely tough interviewer, very business-focused and time-driven. The candidate we rated third in experience did his research and discovered that this hiring manager coached travel baseball like he did and used this commonality to create a connection! They spent forty-five minutes of the one-and-a-half-hour interview (which was scheduled to be just an hour) discussing baseball and mutual contacts. The hiring manager loved this candidate and eventually offered him the job even though there were other finalists with better professional experience. Not all connections are this straightforward, but thankfully there are many ways to establish chemistry.

It is important to practice how to establish chemistry, but it ultimately needs to be seamless and genuine rather than rehearsed. Remember, people are people. Interviewers want to hire (and work with) those they like—never underestimate the power of human connection.

Ways to Build Rapport with Your Interviewer

Before the Interview	During the Interview	After the Interview
Research your interviewer(s) · Google, LinkedIn, personal connections · Take note of common interests · College, previous jobs, place of residence, certifications, hobbies *If all else fails, prepare some general topics* · The weather, how long they've been at the company, local sports teams	*Steal with your eyes* · Look around the room for personal connections, such as pictures of their kids or a hobby, sports memorabilia *Compliment something in the room they might be responsible for* · The layout, a decorative piece	*Get their business card* · Follow-up · In your follow-up email, put something personal you discussed (e.g., "Good luck to your son at his game!" Or, "Hope the Phillies get a win tonight!")

COURTNEY COMMENT

There is a fine line between establishing rapport and being unprofessional. It would be a big mistake to share personal information that could be off putting or skew someone's perception of you as a capable employee (think politics, religion).

I had a friend who tried to establish rapport by discussing her "crazy" sorority days since the interviewer was also a member of Greek life in college. A great connection, but Sunday Funday and hazing is not an appropriate conversation starter when you want to secure a professional position. Rather than seeing her as someone who could be enjoyable to work with, the hiring manager viewed her as immature. She would have been better off discussing their sorority's community involvement and values.

Don't cross the line and you'll do just fine!

21

Acing the Interview
Step 2: The Answers to the Test

O nce you have established chemistry with your interviewer, you should move on to qualifying—this means figuring out exactly what your interviewer is looking for in a new hire. It is important to qualify before the interview gets rolling so you can use the information you receive to answer questions in a more focused manner. The job description for an open position is normally developed by HR using feedback from within the company. What each interviewer is specifically looking for might vary, which is why this step is so important.

Qualifying is like having the answers to the test before you take it!

Qualifying takes finesse and practice. Ask your interviewer an open-ended question to determine what they hope to see. You might say, "I've done research on the company, and I'm excited to be here. I know you're very busy, so to maximize our time together, do you mind sharing with me what you're looking for in a new hire?" Or you might ask, "I've read your job description thoroughly, but I'm curious to understand what's most important to you in a candidate's background for this position?" Practice asking this question in a mirror and aloud so that it feels comfortable.

After asking, listen closely. The first two or three qualities mentioned will often be the most important criteria to that interviewer. When answering their questions, share examples and experiences that reflect those specific traits. At the end of the interview and in follow-up, revisit the criteria and reiterate how you embody those qualities. Qualifying is like having the answers to the test before you take it! And most interviewers will be extremely impressed by the fact that you asked this question. It shows genuine interest and professionalism.

Wondering how to use the information you receive in practice? An example will illustrate it best. I had a candidate who met with three different people at a company in one day. She prepped using the job description but was amazed that when she qualified each interviewer separately, they had unique perspectives. First, HR was looking for specific examples of how she dealt with underperforming direct reports. In this interview, she detailed times she helped employees improve and the steps she took to get them there. She also shared times she exited employees who were not up to the task. Next, her potential direct boss wanted someone with very specific technical skills. With him, she shared specific examples of different software programs she had used and how she could utilize this experience to help the company. Lastly, the CEO wanted to find a team player who was a culture fit. She walked her through different times she had collaborated with others: projects she worked on, mentorship, instances she jumped in to support others. She impressed every interviewer and used the qualifying information to write each one a more personal and targeted thank you email.

Like this candidate, I encourage you to get the answers to the test early on so you can ace the exam!

COURTNEY COMMENT

The idea of qualifying your interviewers is something I never would have thought of on my own, but I think it is genius! I don't doubt that you have many amazing qualities to share, and this process allows you to pick the best ones to highlight for each interviewer.

Qualifying also illustrates how human and genuine the people interviewing us are. It reveals each interviewer's unique thought process. This individuality reminds us that the person across the desk is uniquely human too. What better way to ease interview nerves than a reminder like that?

22

Acing the Interview
Step 3: Ask the Right Questions

The meat and potatoes of any interview is answering questions. In Chapters Twenty-Four to Twenty-Six I go more in-depth about how to answer questions effectively, but the five steps I highlight in these chapters cover the other parts of the interview that are commonly overlooked.

At the end of an interview, you'll be asked if you have any questions. Take the opportunity to ask thoughtful, win-win questions that show preparation and interest. Win-win questions are ones that make the interviewer feel good and help them perceive you positively. Lose-lose questions cast you in a negative light and make the interviewer feel uncomfortable, possibly even defensive. Avoid those completely!

**Asking strong questions will set you apart
from other candidates.**

My son's friend made the mistake of asking lose-lose questions and destroyed multiple job prospects as a result. For example, he asked, "Why has your stock price been going down?" and "I read that your CEO had some personal issues. Can you tell me about that?" These are legitimate concerns, but the time to ask about them is not during a first interview. This young man could have asked these questions in an appropriate and professional manner after receiving an offer. Asking them from the outset made him appear disinterested and put the interviewer in an uncomfortable position. He went on nine interviews with zero offers, even though he had a very strong resume and credentials. Once we planned win-win questions instead, he got the next job he interviewed for!

It is completely appropriate to bring questions you wrote down ahead of time to your interview; share with the interviewer that in preparation you wrote a few questions down, and then take out your notes and choose four to six to ask. What are some strong win-win questions? See below.

1. How will you measure success in this role?

2. If I accomplish all the goals set forth for me, what would a career path here look like?

3. What would I have to accomplish to be considered an overachiever?

4. Can you outline the onboarding process?

5. What could keep me from being successful in this role?

6. What do you like best about working for the company?

7. Is there anything that I can be doing now from a research or reading perspective that might allow me to add value right away?

8. What goals would you have for me in the first thirty days? Ninety? The first year?

9. How would you describe the company culture?

10. A year from now, what will I have had to accomplish for you to feel I was one of the best hires you've made?

I put the questions I feel are strongest first on this list. They will give you insight into the company and more importantly showcase your positive qualities. I encourage you to rephrase the questions in a way that feels comfortable and natural to you. Asking strong questions will set you apart from other candidates, and you always want to take advantage of the opportunity to ask them.

COURTNEY COMMENT

When I interviewed for my first teaching job, I asked a few of these questions (specifically numbers seven and ten), and the interviewers were blown away. They even told me that they had never been asked such thoughtful questions before, and they really appreciated them.

I believe these questions are one reason I stood out as a candidate because they allowed me to appear personal, prepared, and professional.

Be ready to follow through on the answers, though. When I asked what I could be doing over the summer so that I would have a quick start come September, I was given book lists and resources. That was a busy summer!

23

Acing the Interview
Step 4: Any Concerns?

Have you ever been blindsided by a breakup? Shocked by a poor grade on an exam? Surprised by the number on the scale? This is because perception is not necessarily reality. You might have a feeling that something went well or feels right, but that doesn't mean it's true or others had the same experience. This is why you should always ask your interviewer if they have any concerns about your qualifications.

There are many times I've asked a candidate how an interview went, and they believe it went well, while my client disagreed. It's not problematic that concerns exist; it's a reality. I'm actually more alarmed if they don't. *What is problematic is not having the opportunity to hear and address those concerns.*

**It's not problematic that concerns exist....
What is problematic is not having the opportunity
to hear and address those concerns.**

Even if you believe an interview is going well, it's in your best interest to ask if your interviewer has any concerns about your ability to be a good fit. How can you get the interviewer to verbalize their apprehensions? Be conversational and use the opportunity to reiterate your qualifications. For instance, at the conclusion of an interview you might say:

Based on my research about the company prior to this interview, I was really excited about the opportunity to come in today. After our time together here, my interest has only gone up because [insert specific reasons]. You shared that you are looking for someone who is [insert what they want in a new hire], and I think I'm a good fit because [reasons why you are who they are looking for]. Based on my background, do you have any concerns about me adding value in the role?

Then, be incredibly quiet and listen! Hear and understand their concerns.

Common concerns you might come across are that you do not have the proper skillset or experience for the role, there are gaps in your employment, or you are overqualified. Even if the worries are miniscule, the goal is to minimize or overcome them. You want the interviewer to think only positively about you when reflecting on candidates.

One example of needing to minimize a concern would be if an interviewer expresses that they want their new hire to have experience with a certain software, but you have never used it. You cannot overcome this, but you can downplay it:

I understand why you'd feel that way. I haven't used X software, but I have experience using a similar one, Y. If given this opportunity, you won't find anyone who will work harder than I will to learn X. I'll be the first person in every day and the last to leave. All my strengths will overcome the fact that I don't have experience with X, and I will do all I can to fill the knowledge gap.

Here, you validate the concern but minimize its impact by discussing your strengths and willingness to learn.

Further, if a concern is inaccurate, you don't want to be defensive, but you do want to try to help the interviewer move on from it. You might say, "I understand why you feel that way; however, I have not had the opportunity to share with you my experience in that area. I don't think this is a problem because [give a specific example]. Does that alleviate your apprehension?" Here, you give details contrary to their concern and assure that you put the doubt out of their mind.

I once had an executive who met with four people at a company. When we debriefed, he thought the interviews went great; however, he had not asked if there were concerns. The candidate was extremely excited about the job and confident he was going to get it. He even prepared his family for the change. When I debriefed with the client, they said he didn't have enough experience consulting around large scale change initiatives, and they didn't want to extend an offer. If the candidate and client had addressed this together during the interview, the candidate could have overcome the concern by sharing examples where he did this type of work in a previous role. In my opinion, he was the best candidate for them, but that doubt, even though misguided, clouded their perception and they went with someone else. He was prepared to ask if they had any concerns about him, but he didn't think he needed to. It cost him the job.

Take the opportunity to hear concerns and address them on the spot! And when you follow up, it might be appropriate to address them again. In the best-case scenario, you will have resolved all doubt. If nothing else, you'll leave the interview knowing where you stand.

COURTNEY COMMENT

I recommend preparing yourself for the feedback you might get when you do ask this question. It might be difficult to hear. Remind yourself it's typical, and not personal, for your interviewer to have concerns. Take a deep breath before responding so you can reply calmly.

I was able to be the interviewer when I ran the National Honor Society at the school where I work. For students whose qualifications were on the cusp of the guidelines, I asked for more information to determine their eligibility. Were there any other activities they were involved in? Reasons they wanted to be a member of the group? Explanations about grades?

You would be blown away by how many students were offended by the question. I even had a young man tell me he was smarter than all his classmates but didn't feel the need to spend his time studying. He felt he deserved admission more than any of his peers for his natural aptitude. Of course, that response told me all I needed to know.

Then there were the students who owned their missteps, shared their goals, or happily gave more information. This type of reflection and self-awareness highlighted why they deserved this honor.

It was obvious that a student's attitude affected their response to having their credentials questioned, and their response gave me more information than anything else.

I share this because it's a great lesson in humility. The way you approach being questioned will sometimes tell your interviewer even more about you than the concern itself. Do not miss the opportunity to show that you can handle criticism and questioning. That will demonstrate that you are easy to work with, self-aware, and ready to grow.

24

Acing the Interview
Step 5: Closing for the Next Steps

At the conclusion of your interview, make sure you have a clear understanding of the next steps in the process. If you're working with a recruiter, you might be able to find out if you're one of the final candidates and when the next round takes place. Whether you're working with a recruiter or not, you can get some of these details on your own. At the end of your interview you can ask, "So that I can manage my schedule, can you share the next steps of the process and when I can expect to hear back?" They should be able to give you an idea of the timeline.

If you're also interviewing with another company but this one is your first choice, you might word this question differently:

As I shared, my interest in this company has only gone up based on today's meeting. I am talking to another firm who is moving me along quickly, but you're my top choice. I want to manage the process properly; do you mind letting me know your timeline and next steps? I don't want to make any decisions with the other company until I hear back from you.

If the company is interested, they'll respond well. If they don't have a clear answer, they most likely have more concerns than they shared or are scheduled to meet additional candidates.

Asking about next steps will help you understand the timeline and where you stand. It will hopefully help you in the days following the interview. The post-interview anxiety can be overwhelming, but if you know when you'll hear back, you can manage your expectations.

I worked with a candidate who didn't ask about next steps; as a result, she didn't know she was their first interview. They had four more lined up. In person, they gave her positive feedback, so she assumed she was getting the job. Ultimately, they went with someone else. Had she known they had more candidates to interview, she would have been able to keep her expectations in check.

The post-interview anxiety can be overwhelming, but if you know when you'll hear back, you can manage your expectations.

Lastly, I encourage you to gather business cards from everyone you meet while interviewing and follow up with an email to each person within twenty-four hours. Your message should be as personal as possible. Make sure to:

- Thank them for their time
- Express how the interview made your interest in the company increase
- Reiterate specific reasons why you think you're a good fit
- Include a personal tidbit discussed when establishing rapport

This last item is crucial and gives you a better chance of getting a reply. If you do hear back, that's a good sign!

The five steps of interviewing are important to accomplish at every interview. Learn the steps, understand them, and practice them. If you complete all the steps confidently, you most likely did well or understand why you didn't.

When it comes to the job hunt, always remain hopeful. No matter what happens, there will be more opportunities in your future! One bad interview is an opportunity to do better next time.

COURTNEY COMMENT

My dad has prepped many of my friends for interviews, and they *always* get the job when he does. I have heard these steps so many times that I could probably repeat them to you backward in my sleep (which is good, because you need to know them and practice them to do well).

I am young in my career, and I have remained in my school district for years, but I went on many interviews in college and interviewed to transfer within district, join programs, and get summer jobs. I always crush them (thanks, Dad). I have even been told I was the best interview someone ever had.

Trust me, it's not because of my people skills. I'm not here to toot my own horn. I'm lovingly referred to as Awkward Courtney by my friends. I interview well because this process works! Trust it. Practice it. Know it. Do it. And revel in the achievements it brings! You deserve to have options when it comes to taking a job, and these steps will get you there.

25

Responding to "Tell Me About Yourself"

Being caught off-guard by the question, "Tell me about yourself," can be an interviewing recipe for disaster. Many interviewers begin with this question because it is a great icebreaker (and gives the interviewer time to get settled).

Have no fear! I have a few rules to help you navigate this minefield. It's as simple as knowing what information to leave out and what to share. When telling them about yourself, remember:

1. Keep it professional.

An interviewer does not want to know about your personal life at this time. The way this question is phrased might make it feel conversational and personal, but your response should not be. You may believe that using only professional experience to answer this prompt makes you seem uptight or private, but there is a time and place for everything, and an interview setting warrants a career-oriented reply. It's not the time to discuss your family, fraternity, or French bulldog.

An interviewer does not want to know about your personal life at this time.

---

2. Share relevant experience.

Use the information shared by the recruiter or posted in the job description to help craft your response. Answer the prompt by highlighting your relevant work experience.

For example, if the recruiter shares that the company is looking for someone who has experience with SaaS and revitalizing underperforming teams, you want to share your experience in relation to that:

I am a sales manager with a proven track record of exceeding quota and turning around underperforming teams. I have an economics degree from St. John's University and have always had a passion for sales. I actually joined my firm right out of college, and we sell only an SaaS offering. I took over a territory that had never met quota before, and in my first year, I met 128% of quota and earned a spot at their president's conference. In year two, I was promoted to take over the Long Island office. The sales team went from 38% of quota, with only one of nine sales reps qualifying for the company's convention, to 113% of quota, with eight of the nine qualifying for convention. I'm extremely motivated to bring about change and increase revenue.

As you can see, I highlighted the experience that was relevant to what the recruiter shared the firm is looking for. I did not mention that I ran the internship program for the company or that I won the 76ers free-throw competition. Both are fun facts but irrelevant. I did take the opportunity to demonstrate my success. An interview is the time to share your accomplishments if you have the specific data to back it up. The numbers and details are impressive if they pertain to the job spec.

3. Share other ways you're a good fit.

You can also take the opportunity to present yourself as a personality match for the company. Explain specific reasons why you're a good cultural fit:

I enjoy investing in my community. From my research, I see you have a culture of giving back, and that is something I value as well. I volunteer each week at a soup kitchen. I read that you hold quarterly service days, and I would be excited to participate. If given the opportunity to join your team, I look forward to supporting the company's passion for service.

You can also share your professional strengths through excitement over their programs:

I am someone who strives to be the best at what I do. You clearly invest in your people, and I read that you sent four employees to the national consulting conference last year. It is important to me that I constantly hone my craft and grow professionally; I would be honored to take advantage of such opportunities if hired and then share what I learn with my colleagues when I return.

As you can see, I didn't just say I volunteer at a soup kitchen or enjoy professional development. I shared these facts because they connected to the company's goals.

There are many ways to use what you know about the company and role to inform your "tell me about yourself" response.

4. Avoid negativity.

Do not bash your current or past boss. I repeat, do not bash anyone or anything! Those looking for a new role are often unhappy in their current position. That is fair; however, sharing that dissatisfaction with your interviewer is not appropriate. You'll present as a complainer, difficult to work with, and unprofessional. Don't share anything negative about your current company. Stay positive and focus on your accomplishments.

5. Rehearse your response.

This step is crucial. Prepare your response. Record yourself saying it. Play it over and over again so that it becomes natural. If you don't, you may freeze on the spot or end up rambling—you want to avoid both!

Being asked to tell your interviewer about yourself is easy if you're prepared. More importantly, it's an opportunity! Now that you know it might come up, you can make sure you're ready and don't waste the chance to sell yourself!

COURTNEY COMMENT

The most uncomfortable and beneficial experience of my job search history is when my dad sat in on one of my video interviews. I knew the five-step process, did my research, and had loads of notes. It was also one of my first interviews right out of college, and my nerves were at an all-time high.

Because it was a Skype interview, my dad offered to listen and give feedback. I agreed, as long as he sat out of the interviewer's sightline (and mine too!). This was my first mistake.

The opening question was, "Tell me about yourself." And guess what? My dad forgot to prepare me for that one! He started writing notes in large letters on computer paper to hold up for me in front of the laptop screen. But it was too late. I went on to ramble about how I love hiking and climbed Mt. Kilimanjaro. Mistake number two. Too personal!

After the interview, we workshopped a future response so that I would be prepared for this question next time, but that first fail and my dad holding up the scribbled notes (which he did multiple times over that hour) is etched in my memory forever.

26

Responding to "Why Us?"

Overprepare. It's the key to success in life and interviewing! There are many predictable parts of an interview, and one of those parts is being asked, "Why are you interested in our company?" How do you respond? You don't want to wing it, so you're already ahead of the curve by reading this chapter. Conquering this question means preparing an answer unique to each company, which starts with research.

Simply put—do your research!

If you share specific reasons why you respect the company and why you are excited about the opportunity, you will be perceived as professional and serious about the job. On the other hand, if you cannot answer this question clearly, they might assume you'll also fail to prepare and put in the appropriate effort if hired. Your answer could dictate whether or not you receive an offer.

I recommend that you start your research at the company's website. Review it to get an understanding for how they present themselves, the industry, and their values. The most important section is "About Us." What matters to them? What is their mission statement? Who do they work with? Who do they hire? You'll find a lot of the answers there. If they have a blog, read the posts to find out what interests them and their employees. If they have newsletters, subscribe so you have their most timely news. Working with a recruiter? Gather information that way too. Google the company and find them on social media. Know their competitors. Know how they are doing in the marketplace. If it's a startup, use Crunchbase to access information on funding, acquisitions, and even message boards. If you have had a chance to ask the interviewer what attracted them to the company, you can use that information as well.

If available, access the company's stock price from the most recent quarter, read the CEO's quarterly statements, and dig into investor relations. Want to really impress them? Use LinkedIn to connect with the people who you will meet. Learn their backgrounds and see if you have any similar work history or connections. If there are alumni from your same college at the company, reach out to them and get advice and information. That person can be a champion for you on the inside.

Once you gather all the information available, see what aligns with your own values. Obviously, anything negative that you uncover about the company should not be used here. Think about the big takeaways from your research. It might even help to write down the "top three" big ideas to help you focus your response.

Think:

- What ideas came up again and again?
- What are the company's values?
- What do they do that's unique?
- What are they proud of?
- What about them speaks to who I am?

Now you are ready to draft your response about why you want to work there.

Here are some ideas to help you phrase your answer:

- When I read your mission statement, I immediately connected with...
- The culture of the firm is apparent through X, and I love Y. I would fit in so well because...

- When researching the company, what impressed me most was X (e.g., how you keep introducing new products). It excited me because...
- I read an article about your company being X (e.g., ahead of the curve and innovative). I really connected with that because...
- You are growing dramatically, and at a pace I believe I could thrive in because...
- I wasn't looking to make a career move, but I was contacted by X, and they told me Y. That really made me want to come in and meet with you.
- I am very excited about your...

Notice that when I phrase these responses, I make it clear that I did my research. Referring to their mission statement or other pieces of data or articles that you read makes it clear that you prepared. That will set you apart from other potential new hires as someone who is passionate, excited, and professional.

COURTNEY COMMENT

Research is something we younger people excel in, and that gives us an edge. So, get on that iPhone or tablet and do what twenty-some-things do best—cyberstalk! Any piece of information might come in handy, and I know you'll uncover it all.

Where to start? Beyond the website and stock price, you can look up the company on social media and take note of what they post because it will show you what they value. Do this process with the names of executives at the company as well. Look for common trends and topics in the content. Just like you'd do for a potential Tinder date, uncover all you can beforehand!

When you research the company, you also learn more about whether it's a good fit for you, and that information can help you make the right decision once you do get the offer!

27

Understanding Behavioral Interviewing

As previously mentioned, your responses to the interviewer's questions are the most consequential aspect of the interview. This chapter is longer because it explains the behavioral interviewing process, shares sample questions, gives a model response, and overviews common mistakes. There is a lot of information, so I suggest reading it slowly, section by section.

A popular type of interviewing style is the behavioral interview approach. This is a research-based process that allows a team of interviewers to focus on an applicant's relevant work history. It uses past performance to predict future success. The rationale is that an applicant who hasn't demonstrated a necessary skill in their previous position won't be likely to do so at your firm. Companies use this method because it takes the emotion out of the hiring process and puts the spotlight on real experience.

Prior to an interview, you should research the company to see if they use a behavioral interview approach; regardless, this method is a strong way to prepare interview responses for any type of interview and can be helpful in various professional situations. When you arrive at an interview that utilizes the behavioral method, the interviewer will overview what to expect and explain that they're looking for your specific work-related experiences that demonstrate particular skills.

Once you have been interviewed by everyone on the hiring team, a meeting is scheduled to debrief and integrate data. The group discusses the candidates, the skills assessed, questions asked, responses, and how they rated each applicant. The hiring team does not discuss potential new hires until the debrief, so each skills assessment is fair and independent. There are no gut decisions; the team uses data to make the final decision. They won't always choose the highest-scored candidate, but the data helps them narrow down the list and make a rational decision. How can you prepare to be at the top of that list? This chapter will show you.

Past performance predicts future success.

Before the Interview

Before going in to meet the interviewers, identify what skills you think are most important to be successful in the role. List specific examples of how you've demonstrated proficiency in each of these areas.

Prepare many different examples. Look back at your past performance documents and appraisals for ideas. Regardless of whether you use all the examples you find, this process can boost your confidence, create a repertoire of strong work experience, and remind you of your successes.

Commonly Assessed Skills

Many of the proficiencies you'll be asked about are soft skills, which relate to your people skills:

- Collaboration and Teamwork
- Time Management
- Adaptability (i.e., problem-solving)
- Client-Facing Skills (e.g., difficult customers)
- Initiative and Enthusiasm

- Communication
- Motivation and Values (i.e., work ethic and ethos)
- Conflict Resolution

Commonly Asked Questions

Many of the questions will start with the phrase, "Tell me about a time…" or "Give me an example of…" Here are a few sample questions:

1. Can you give me an example of a goal reached and how it was achieved?

   (Time Management)

2. What do you do when your schedule gets interrupted?

   (Ability to Adapt)

3. Tell me about a time you had to handle a difficult situation with a coworker.

   (Communication)

4. Tell me about a time you had to work with a team to complete a project on time. What was your input?

   (Collaboration and Teamwork)

5. Tell me about a time there was a difficult customer and how you handled it.

   (Client-Facing Skills)

6. Give me an example of a time you demonstrated initiative.

   (Initiative)

7. Give me an example of a time you were able to be creative with your work. What was exciting or difficult about it?

   (Motivation and Values)

8. Give me an example of a time when you had to think on your feet in order to remove yourself from a difficult or awkward situation.

   (Ability to Adapt)

The STAR Technique

My past client, DDI (Developmental Dimensions International), is credited with a technique called the STAR Method, which helps you craft your responses. This technique assists you in staying focused, concise, and specific. STAR stands for:

Situation

Task

Action

Result

When answering an interview question, overview each of these parts in a response that is **no longer than two minutes**. DDI groups S and T together, but I separate them in my explanation.

Situation What is the situation you were in? Set the stage for the story. Keep it short and simple.
Task Describe the goal at hand. Keep it concise and extremely specific.
Action Explain the actions you took to overcome the challenge; focus on your individual contribution. This should be the most in-depth portion of the response.
Result Describe the outcome of your efforts. For impact, quantify the results. You can also share how you grew because of the situation. Be brief and focused.

When sharing a scenario where your original result was not what you had hoped for and therefore tried an alternative action, use STAR/**AR** and tag on a second action and result.

Example STAR Response

Question: Tell me about a time when you had to work with a difficult customer.
Targeted Skills: Initiative and Client-Relations
Situation I had a customer that placed an order for a custom engine but wanted it sooner than our typical timeline allows. I was upfront that the engine would take five to six weeks to deliver, but he called daily to inquire about the delivery date.
Task I wanted to find a way to keep the customer happy, manage expectations, and also see if I could speed up the timeline.
Action I used communication to stay in constant contact with the key players in my company, the manufacturing plant, and the client. Because the engine was custom, I was consistently told there was a five-to-six-week timeline, and I had to relay this message to the client again. When communicating back to the client, I made sure I was respectful and clear that I was doing all that I could to deliver it earlier. I commiserated with him and assured him that I understood his needs so that he felt heard. I kept a log of all communication so that I could keep track of everything and stay honest. Eventually, on week three, I found out the product was ready to ship on one of my calls to the manufacturer. There was no email notification, but because I called twice a week to check in, I found out immediately. I then was able to find a special delivery service to get the client the product the next day.
Result As a result of my initiative and communication, I delivered the engine in under four weeks rather than five or six. The customer was very happy and assured me that he would use us again for their next order, which he did.

Notice that the above response uses the word "I" often and focuses on the individual's involvement in the task (not the manufacturer's or boss's). The individual did not talk poorly about the customer, and the response is concise and specific with relevant details. Finally, the answer directly states the targeted skills. This is what to aim for!

Common Missteps

There are some common mistakes to avoid when answering behavioral questions.

1. **Problem:** You can't think of a good example, so you wing it.

   Solution: To avoid rambling about random work experience (and score poorly), buy yourself more time to reflect. Say, "Great question. Can we come back to it? I want to think about it and make sure I answer thoughtfully."

2. **Problem:** You talk about the team more than yourself.

   Solution: Don't be modest! To avoid this, use "me" and "I" statements instead of "us" and "we." The interviewers want to know about your specific role in a collaborative project.

3. **Problem:** You share more examples from college or your personal life than your career.

   Solution: Focus on professional examples. Stick with your work experience, although at times, academic situations or volunteer work could apply.

4. **Problem:** Your example is irrelevant.

   Solution: Make sure you stay on task. Do not try to make an example work if it's not related to the question. To avoid this, repeat the prompt throughout your response.

5. **Problem:** Your example demonstrates a negative trait.

   Solution: Do not share any information that might trouble the interviewer because they may fixate on it. Only share a failure if it does not highlight a poor personality trait and you can show how you grew as a result. It is better to stick to win-win scenarios.

6. **Problem:** You lie.

   Solution: Do not create stories. It will undermine your credibility, which will come back to hurt you if hired. It can also make you appear disingenuous.

Overall, behavioral interviews can be overwhelming. They take preparation; however, when you do prepare, you become more confident. Use the STAR chart to write out responses to prepare for your interview and then practice saying them aloud. Be open and honest, and you'll present yourself and your skills effectively. If past performance predicts future success, you simply need to be sincere and share all your incredible accomplishments!

COURTNEY COMMENT

I like to come up with my best examples ahead of time and practice describing them using STAR. Then, I think of how many questions each scenario can be used to answer.

For example, I might wish to discuss the time that I worked with an English language learner to overcome her fear of public speaking by helping her build confidence to present a scene from a play. I would write this scenario down using the STAR method and then brainstorm the types of questions I could use the scenario to answer. What could it be used to showcase? My flexibility, classroom culture, student achievement, and more.

I aim to go into an interview with four or five examples like this one planned out using STAR. I keep in mind how I can use each one to illustrate various skills, and it helps me excel when I'm in the hot seat. Take the time to do this, too. Trust me, it's worth it!

28

Should You Take the Job?

Once you receive a job offer, you must assess the position to assure that it's the right move for you. How do you evaluate the company and the opportunity? I believe this process starts *before* the offer is made. Actually, it starts before the interview itself. Throughout the interview process, I encourage you to take notes on what's attracting you to the job and the company based upon what you read, the people you meet, and the way you feel. Also keep track of your questions and concerns.

RCI uses a "Reasons Why" document with each candidate to keep a record of this information throughout the process and reflect with candidates before they decide to accept an offer. I encourage you to do this too! It helps you avoid trying to fit a square peg into a round hole. There should be many reasons why you want to take a position. Money alone is never enough. If you are unable to list enough positives, it's a sign that the job is probably not for you. See below for some examples of reasons why you might consider accepting a new position.

Possible "Reasons Why"

· Can grow and take on more responsibility	· More services than current firm
· Opportunity to expand your professional knowledge	· Higher base salary
· Company's training is advanced, and you can grow professionally	· Quicker promotion track
· Less (or more) travel	· Better benefits that cost less
· Strong boss you can learn from and who will invest in you	· Longer parental leave
· Core values align with yours	· Company has a pension
· 401(k) match is 50%	· They are excited about me
· Additional week vacation	· I'll be part of the leadership team
· Work from home twice a week	· I'll have a big voice in the room
· Shorter commute	· My input will be valued
· Take on two biggest clients	· Can recruit my own team
	· Welcoming and collegial culture
	· Quarterly bonuses

I had a candidate who had two reasons why she wanted to take a job, and those reasons were weak. We discussed it at length, and she eventually shared that she wasn't happy in her current company and would take anything that came her way. This was a major concern for me as a recruiter. I coached her to be careful and resist jumping in too quickly. Because she did not have strong reasons why she wanted this particular role, she kept looking until she found an opportunity she was absolutely certain about. She ultimately took a role that was a long-term fit; her list of "Reasons Why" was extensive and convincing. She remained there for a long time and was promoted every few years.

I want you to *know* a job is the right match for you. Accepting a job offer should never be a leap of faith; it should be a rational, informed decision. As a final step, I suggest asking yourself the following three questions before taking the job:

1. Can I add value to the organization and contribute meaningfully to its success?

No matter your position or level, it's important to feel that your work is purposeful and supports a larger objective. When that's not the case, problems crop up.

I still remember the candidate Bob who accepted a Chief Sales Officer position, assuming he could add value by expanding the sales force and recommending product development. The CEO, on the other hand, wanted him to maintain the status quo (he was interested in selling the company, necessitating keeping profits high). The issue here is that the candidate and the CEO did not discuss their desires and objectives. When I confronted the CEO about the mismatch, he explained that if the candidate had asked the right questions, he would have responded honestly. Shortly after, and disappointed to say the least, Bob left to take a job where he could make an impact.

2. In what ways will I grow professionally from taking this position?

While it's important to support your employer and further their objectives, it's equally important that you work toward your own professional goals. Will you gain new skills? Will the work give you a sense of satisfaction? Is it too easy? Will you become bored and want to leave far too soon? A year after accepting the role, you should be able to identify exactly how you've grown as a result of taking a specific position.

Accepting a job offer should never be a leap of faith; it should be a rational, informed decision.

---

3. How do I honestly feel about the people that make up the organization, especially my immediate boss?

The most important relationship is with the person you report to. You must respect this person and the knowledge they can share, as well as feel a personal connection. If you like the person you work for, you'll want to stay there long-term. Try to get a good feeling for the person who will be your boss.

I placed a candidate over twenty years ago in the consulting practice at a big four accounting firm. Although the job is demanding and stressful, the candidate is still there today, mainly because of his relationship with his first manager. Now one of his best friends, this manager has promoted him three different times!

Likewise, it's critical that you have positive relationships with your coworkers, especially the people you rub elbows with daily. Try to connect with the people you will work with before you take a job. If you feel "at odds" with them, your work life can become challenging! Don't forget that you spend eight hours or more a day with these people. If you have a problem tolerating Crazy Uncle Jerry for a couple of hours every Thanksgiving, think what working with Crazy Charlie five days a week can do to your psyche over time.

Whether it's your first job out of college or your next C-Level role, before accepting any new position, make sure you have many reasons why it's right for you and that you can answer these three questions comfortably and confidently.

COURTNEY COMMENT

These are powerful questions. Are you kicking yourself that you didn't explore them *before* taking your current position?

Take a moment now to ask yourself, should I *keep* my current job? Am I happy, challenged, and satisfied? Many of us feel stuck because of financial insecurity, habit, or general fear. Many tips in this book will help you find the right next move for you so that you don't need to stay somewhere that isn't fulfilling. You have to be willing to make that change!

When we were ready to have our baby, Rich and I knew his current role would not work for our family. He started a job search (very scary while your wife's bump is expanding in diameter each week) and made sure there would be many "reasons why" as well as clear answers to the three questions as he explored different roles. He was offered a job that would be a lateral move with a slightly lower salary, but the option to work from home part-time, a much shorter commute, a quicker chance for upward mobility, a collegial atmosphere, an opportunity to wear multiple hats, and an executive team that genuinely cares about him and work-life balance made accepting the offer a no-brainer. And as a family, we have never looked back! It is the information in the chapter above that helped make this the best one for us.

29

Negotiating the Offer

You have received a verbal offer and now it's time to celebrate! Well, almost.

Determining whether a job offer is right for you is important, and if your "Reasons Why" lead to a "no," then you should follow that path. Turn down the offer respectfully and responsibly by being extremely complimentary and concise. You can say, "I really enjoyed getting to know your people, and I admire the culture here. After much review, I feel that there is more I need to accomplish in my current role, so I have to decline the offer at this time." Or, "I appreciate your time and interest, but I have decided to go in a different direction."

You cannot lose by asking for more favorable items.

If you evaluate your "Reasons Why" and determine you do want to accept a new role, you are in a great position! You have made it to the end of the race and the trophy is within reach. But which trophy will you get? That depends upon how you negotiate the offer.

If your offer is verbal, first ask to have the terms put in writing. This concrete outline will help you negotiate. At this point, the company officially wants you and has formalized its offer; you are now in the driver's seat.

It will not impact how the company feels about you to negotiate the deal, as long as you do so in a professional manner. I promise you that they will not rescind the offer; in fact, they will respect you for asking. I repeat, they will not retract your offer! You cannot lose by asking for more favorable terms (given you do so humbly).

Before deciding which terms to negotiate, I suggest you discuss the proposed offer with business-minded people who care about you. Be sure your chosen confidantes will give you the best advice and have no hidden agendas. Don't accept your offer until you receive input from others and discuss the terms.

I also recommend that, if possible, you ask to spend half a day at the company before negotiating or accepting an offer. While there, have all your questions answered and observe. What is it really like to be in the shoes of an employee there? Sit with people. Ask yourself, *Can I see myself doing this? Can I see myself being happy and successful here?* Whether or not you go in for an observation day, make sure you have asked all outstanding questions and addressed all remaining concerns. Clear up any and all doubts.

At this point, if you still want to accept the offer, I encourage you to negotiate the terms. Include three parts in your response to the initial offer:

1. To open the conversation, reiterate your excitement and confidence in the company:

   "I am so excited about the company and the role. I know I can be successful because…."

2. Then, bring up any potential concerns—for example, salary-related concerns:

   "I was hoping for a little higher salary because other companies I am talking with are offering me more."

   Or you can give a more specific reason for a salary bump:

   "I would have to move to the city for this position, and I am ready to do so, but my cost of living will be much higher, so I was hoping for a higher base."

3. End with helping the company feel confident in your commitment to them:

"If you are able to work with me on this, I am prepared to resign from my current role and start at my new position on [insert specific date]."

If the company cannot give you a higher base salary, there are other ways to increase the offer. You want to discuss these options. Explain that you understand their situation and would love to find a way to join the team. This might be in the form of a signing bonus, a pro-rated bonus, or an earlier review so that your salary increases sooner. Politely ask if any of these options would be possible to help close the salary gap. Or perhaps they can offer perks such as an extra week vacation. Explore possibilities they may be open to.

Hopefully, you can negotiate the offer to receive a bit more compensation or other such benefits. If not, no harm done, and you can be sure that you are getting the best possible offer at this time. And you still have an exciting new opportunity to accept. Now it's time to celebrate!

COURTNEY COMMENT

The last offer my husband accepted, the company was unable to offer him a higher salary. They were already offering him the highest part of the salary range. They did work with him though and gave him a signing bonus, paid after ninety days. We were so happy that he asked, and of course, we went out for drinks on that ninetieth day! More importantly, he felt valued.

Unfortunately, as a state employee, I do not have this same opportunity to negotiate my compensation or benefits. I am lucky to be protected by a union though that assures I am treated fairly.

30

Resigning Professionally and Navigating the Counteroffer

You have an offer to accept, and you are positive that it is the right move for you. You have done your due diligence, completed your "Reasons Why" list, answered the three critical questions, and addressed your concerns. You have negotiated the offer and signed the employment contract. You have your start date, and your life is about to begin anew! But there is one raincloud hanging over your head—your resignation. Navigating your resignation and possibly a counteroffer is the final step in securing your next big role.

Do not entertain any counteroffers.

To effectively resign, work through the following steps:

1. Leave on a positive note.

Approach your resignation from your current company with the assumption that one day you will need them to be a reference. It is essential that you leave on good terms. This is not the time to tell the company everything they did wrong or to air your grievances. That might be cathartic in the moment, but it can hurt you in the future. Be polite and positive.

2. Formally submit a resignation letter.

Some people like to make their direct boss aware of their resignation in person and off-the-record initially. If this feels right for you, do so. Just be prepared for a counteroffer and see step three for how to navigate that.

Whether you tell your boss verbally or not, you will need to submit a formal resignation letter. This letter should be addressed to your boss and cc Human Resources. The resignation letter should be brief, give two weeks' notice, and stay professional. It is also important to assure them in writing that your decision is final. Express that you are willing to help transition your role in any way needed. See a sample resignation letter at the end of this chapter.

3. Leave no room for a counteroffer.

Once you have submitted the resignation letter, your boss will want to meet with you. If you are a valued employee, they will try to convince you to change your mind. By resigning, you ultimately make your boss's job more difficult (your boss will have to manage your responsibilities in the short term, interview and hire your replacement, and train the replacement). This may result in them doing and saying anything to keep you.

Don't go there; do not entertain any counteroffers.

In my experience, if you allow your current company to offer you more money and give them time to try and talk you into staying but you still leave, you can hurt your employer's feelings, and it reflects poorly on you.

Instead, share that you really appreciate their sentiments, but your mind is made up. Verbalize the finality of your decision. Do not waste their time.

Your boss may want you to talk to their boss, and you should respectfully do so, but you must be clear that your mind is made up and reiterate that throughout those conversations.

If you think your company can offer you more money or a title change that would make you want to stay, discuss that before the resignation and before you sign an offer somewhere else. This part of the process is not the appropriate time to entertain that idea, and you should have your mind set on leaving when you make the company aware of your resignation.

4. Only share information about your new role if you are comfortable.

You do not have to tell your current company who you are going to work for. Do not feel pressured. If asked, you can simply respond, "The company asked me to keep it confidential. Once I start and can tell you, I will, but I can't right now." Then they shouldn't press further.

They might also ask you for your new title and say that they can match that or do better. Again, do not open that door! It never ends well if you have your mind set on leaving.

5. Fight the guilt.

There is no reason for you to feel badly about a resignation. If your boss is offered a better opportunity, they would most likely pursue it too. If your boss needed to make budget cuts and eliminate your position, they would do that as well. Just like anyone else, you must make the best professional decision for you. You should not feel guilty. This is a time to celebrate.

If you thoughtfully concluded that leaving is the right move, then that is the decision to stick with! Top executives and HR specialists estimate anywhere from 75-95% of people who accept counteroffers end up leaving the company within a year.[1] Why? The company sometimes begins to question your loyalty. More profoundly, even though the role or the compensation might change after a counteroffer, the reasons you originally wanted to leave remain.

---

[1] Kelly O. Klay, "How To Leave A Job Gracefully," San Francisco: Heidrick & Struggles International, Inc., 2017, https://www.heidrick.com/Knowledge-Center/Publication/How_to_leave_a_job_gracefully. Last accessed July 30, 2021.

If it takes a resignation for your company to pay you what you're worth or promote you, what does that really say? They felt okay taking advantage of you up to this point.

I once placed a candidate who had to resign from one of the big four consulting firms; she was one level below partner and their highest rated managing director. She started a mentorship program for mothers on maternity leave to transition back slowly and successfully, and she was a mentor herself to many young women. She was highly respected but unhappy because she had no work-life balance, and the work that she loved was only a small portion of the company's business. Contrarily, the firm she signed an offer with had a strong culture for work-life balance, and their primary focus reflected her professional passions. She had seventeen reasons why she wanted the job and had all her questions answered. When she went to resign, her boss told her that he was not accepting her resignation. He sent her to his boss, who also refused to accept her resignation and insulted the company she was leaving them for (which only further cemented that she made the right choice). He sent her to speak to *his* boss, even though she had been clear that her decision was final. His boss told her that she was locked in to become partner that year, and he showed her what she would earn over the next ten years, but still, she did not change her mind. In the end, the CEO called her personally to show support and assure her that if she ever regretted leaving, they would want her back, which really impressed me as a business professional.

This experience shows how difficult it is to resign when you're a real superstar. But because the candidate was sure of her decision and honest and respectful with the company, she was able to properly navigate it. In her new role, she has been promoted twice and is a senior partner leading one of their practices. She never doubted the move. Just like her, you can successfully resign and change your life and career for the better.

Sample Resignation Letter

Date

Your Name
Your Address
Recipient Name
Title
Organization
Address

Dear [Insert Supervisor's Name],

I was contacted about a position and decided to explore it further. After much consideration, I have decided to resign from my position at [insert company name] effective upon [insert date two weeks from when letter is sent].

It was not an easy decision, but it is a final decision.

I will do whatever I can to make this transition as easy as possible for the firm.

I hope you feel as positive about my X years with the company as I do. I want to thank you for your support and guidance.

Sincerely,

Signature
Typed Name
Date

cc: HR Manager

COURTNEY COMMENT

The thought of resigning puts a pit in my stomach! I hate the feeling of letting people down, especially coworkers or students.

That is why the "guilt-free" advice and reasoning above is so important to remember. If you resign professionally, you have nothing to feel bad about. Anyone in your situation would take a better opportunity as well.

But ugh, why is the pit still there?! Again, some things are just easier said than done. If you are resigning and feel the guilt too, give yourself grace, know it's normal, but still make the best decision for you and your family.

PART THREE

CAREER

31

Find Your Purpose

How do you build a lasting career? This is the million-dollar question, and if I had a simple formula to share, I'd be the owner of a professional sports team by now. I can give you a general formula, but it's far from simple:

Passion + Salary + Strong Management + Culture and Climate +
Skillset + Unicorns....

I think you get the point. There are many factors that will affect your ultimate career success and longevity. What do I believe is the most impactful of the ingredients over the trajectory of your working life? Passion!

**"The two most important days in your life are the day
you are born and the day you find out why."**

—MARK TWAIN

If you have passion for the work that you do and you enjoy doing it, you won't ever wake up feeling as though you're going to a job. Mark Twain said, "The two most important days in your life are the day you are born and the day you find out why." I agree wholeheartedly with the importance he places on finding your "why." Knowing your purpose transforms your life and sets you on a path to feeling satisfied with who you are.

This is not an easy accomplishment in a country that values salary and position over happiness. How many people do you know that choose a career path based upon title and compensation? Are they satisfied? In my experience, the ones who follow a passion above all else are the most fulfilled and therefore successful. Since you spend more time at work than you do anywhere else, imagine how job dissatisfaction would negatively impact your health and relationships. You deserve better!

What does it mean to follow your passion? Find something you love doing and find a way to make a living doing it. Just going through the motions of a job to collect a paycheck results in negativity, stagnancy, and overall dissatisfaction. On the other hand, following your interests will lead you to long-term professional success: promotions, strong business relationships, and pride in your work.

Let's take a look at Bill from one of the big four accounting firms. He was a director who had a real passion for consulting in the leadership and talent management space, and he loved being a coach. However, he was frustrated because his current role was primarily focused on technology consulting. Bill took this advice, and I hope you do too—if you are unhappy, make a change. We helped him find a role as an associate partner where he could consult in leadership and talent management daily. The result? In eighteen months, he was promoted to senior partner; one year later, he was running one of their largest verticals. When you are fulfilled, there is a much greater chance for success.

Similarly, my brother-in-law was a lawyer with a Ph.D. in political science. He spent years in school, but when he started practicing law with a prestigious law firm in New York City, he quickly realized he was unhappy; it was draining his energy to show up to the office each day. He could have stayed on this career path, and many people advised him to do just that since he spent years of his life and hundreds of thousands of dollars on his education. From a practical standpoint, he was making a great deal of money, but he was miserable. He took a risk and went in a completely different direction. He started a company where he could be more creative, developing apps and children's toys. He now has six kids and a successful career to support his family, while also experiencing meaning and joy.

Unlike my brother-in-law, you can save time and money if you make sure the reality of a job matches your expectation of it before committing to a certain professional path. It's easy to fall in love with the idea of a job rather than the actuality of it. Before declaring a major, complete internships and shadow people in the field. Courtney thought she wanted to pursue law and completed a summer internship at a boutique law firm to expose herself to all parts of the field—paperwork, research, arbitration, the courtroom, and so on. By the end of the summer, she had a good idea of what it was like to be a lawyer, and that's why she's now a teacher.

Make sure you pursue a career path that truly gives you life, and you will be unstoppable! Find a vocation rather than an occupation, and you will have unlocked the key to success (no unicorns needed).

COURTNEY COMMENT

This is advice that is so easy to understand but so difficult to implement. At least for me. As a competitive person, I believed I needed to follow my head rather than my heart when choosing a career path. But my head was so convoluted. It was muddled with misconceptions about which careers were so-called respectable and which professions paid the highest salaries. Maybe this was because of the population of the high school and college I attended, which was predominantly white and affluent, or maybe it was because we live in a capitalistic country, or maybe it was a little bit of both.

I attended Lehigh University and double majored in English and economics. I loved reading and writing but wanted to prove I could succeed in business: at Lehigh, liberal arts were laughable. There, I was on the precipice of my future with half of me following my head, an economics degree, and the other half of me following my heart, English. I saw success in both majors, but economics felt like work! English? I spent nights curled up with books and hours researching and writing, happily typing away and excited to share my thoughts in discussion. My extracurricular activities included tutoring and mentoring programs. If there was a chance to help others, I was there because it made me happy and gave me purpose. Still, I thought I needed to be "better."

So I interned for my dad one summer, and another summer I spent at a law firm. I was miserable. Thank goodness for internships because they allowed me to make the best choice. My thoughts might have been muddled, but my hands-on experience sure wasn't.

I eventually put my pride aside and followed my heart. My work with my students gives me life, and I am so happy each morning to walk into my classroom rather than an office building.

As for the money? I might not be a millionaire, but who said that's the only way to measure success?

32

Take the Stairs

Anything in life worth doing is worth doing to the best of your ability. Having passion for your work is essential, and when combined with work ethic, the sky's the limit. Zig Ziglar said it best: "There is no elevator to success. You have to take the stairs." Put another way, there's no easy or fast way to advance in your career. You must do the work.

A young woman named Nicole started at my company in pursuit of a new career path. Nicole struggled a great deal in the beginning because she had no prior search experience, but I was never concerned about her future success. Why? She was the first one in the office every morning with a list of questions, and she was one of the last to leave each night. She had high daily activity and worked hard to understand every part of the job. I knew she would be a superstar because she threw herself into the role. Now, she is one of our top performers. She took the stairs!

Another example of the power of drive comes from Ryan Arcidiacono, a young man I coached in AAU basketball who also completed the RCI internship program. Ryan was always the first on the court and stayed after practice to take a certain number of shots on his own. I've never seen someone more determined. The payoff? A full scholarship to Villanova, MVP of the 2016 NCAA March Madness Tournament, and now an NBA player for the Chicago Bulls. He's not the tallest or the fastest, but he will outwork anyone.

"There is no elevator to success. You have to take the stairs."

—ZIG ZIGLAR

The above examples highlight certain traits that promote success:

- Being early and staying late
- Asking questions
- Resilience
- Focus

Your work ethic is what will set you apart from others in your career. If you focus on what you can control and go above and beyond whenever possible, your boss will want to help you when you do struggle. If you take the stairs, you will find yourself at the top, and you'll be better for it. Those who take the elevator? They often get stuck on a lower floor.

COURTNEY COMMENT

If you outwork others, you will be a precious commodity. It's my work ethic that got me to where I am today. You know those people in your high school classes that never needed to study and always got the A? That wasn't me. I was the one hitting the books. And I think I'm better for it. It's this tenacity that helps me achieve my goals.

You won't have to pull all-nighters the rest of your life, but you need to be willing to do so as you work your way to the top. No one will hand you your dream job and let you roll out of bed at nine in the morning, make the same mistakes twice, or miss deadlines.

With solid effort, you can accomplish your career goals, but you have to make them happen.

33

Seek Out a Mentor

There is a certain insight that comes with time and practice. It brings a unique perspective that can only come from someone who has lived life longer. All of us, especially young people, can benefit from the guidance of someone older, a mentor, to help navigate life's complexities. With experience comes wisdom and knowledge.

There is...a unique perspective that can only come from someone who has lived life longer.

This person is known as a Dutch uncle. The term can be traced back to the early 1800s as an allusion to the Dutch being blunt, practical, and outspoken. Who doesn't need someone who will give us the cold, hard truth? Your Dutch uncle is not a parent but is someone older who sincerely cares about you and believes in you. They have no hidden agendas and will give honest feedback and advice, whether you want to hear it or not.

To find this person, identify someone to whom you feel a connection. This might be someone who has helped you in the past or someone in the shoes you wish to fill one day. The Dutch uncle is especially helpful when it comes to your career. You will be surprised by the kindness of those more accomplished in your field and their desire to help young professionals just starting out.

When I began my career in corporate America, my mentor was a man I greatly respected named Ralph, the General Manager of Alcatel's New York office. I wanted to be in a similar role one day. He believed in me, gave me my first promotion, and always prioritized me when I needed career advice, even after I left Alcatel.

The first big promotion I was offered was from sales manager in Long Island to general manager in Atlanta. The marketplace was strong, the current GM was being promoted, the region was performing well, and I'd manage operations for the first time—a big step up! But I was hesitant because it would be a major relocation for my family and take us away from our relatives. Ralph's advice was sound: 1. I would have other opportunities, and 2. The best I could do in Atlanta was maintain or modestly grow the territory (it was already high performing).

Everyone else advised me to jump at the opportunity while Ralph understood my strengths, the industry, and my career goals. My peers were young and money-hungry, whereas Ralph knew the moves that would help me achieve my long-term goals; taking this promotion was playing it too safe. With Ralph's guidance, I turned the Atlanta role down and accepted a promotion a few months later as the GM of New Jersey, the lowest performing Alcatel branch in the country. As Ralph put it, I had nowhere to go but up, and the challenge would showcase my skillset. The branch became number one in the country, we stayed within ninety minutes of our extended family, and I was on the trajectory that eventually led to owning my own business.

If you're lucky enough to find your Ralph, understand that it's your responsibility to foster and cultivate the relationship. Stay in touch, update your mentor on your career, and be humble and gracious. Take them out for dinner and remember them on holidays.

Another important aspect of the mentor/mentee relationship is being receptive to advice. A national trainer in the search industry, Lou Scott, was involved with the same franchise as me. On an awards trip, I took the opportunity to ask if he had any advice for me. Surprisingly, he'd been following my career and was impressed with my success. But (why is there always a *but*?), he thought I cursed too much, which gave people a poor impression of me. I was initially taken aback; I wasn't even aware of the habit. As I started to take note of my language, I realized he was right. From that point on, I made a concerted effort not to swear, and to this day I rarely curse. That honest feedback was critical and being open to it was even more important.

Soak up all you can from those who are more experienced. These are the people who will help you find the success you desire, and they will be the ones you remember (and who are cheering you on) when you do achieve your dreams.

COURTNEY COMMENT

My Dutch uncle was a woman named Carolyn Evans. She was an amazing, retired English teacher and department head with a sincere passion for teaching. I met her as my college professor, a later-in-life endeavor that allowed her to transition from a lifetime in the classroom to training those who would fill her shoes. I knew she was the right mentor for me because she focused on the overwhelming positives of the profession, and she believed in my ability to be an impactful teacher. Whether it be over tea at her house or late night after class, she always had time and honest advice.

To this day, I channel her energy into who I am as a colleague and teacher. She baked for her college students, and now I never arrive to a big meeting empty-handed. I realize the value of food when it comes to making a group feel like a family. She shared that she would have her colleagues over for wine by the pool to work on lesson plans during the summer, and I too try to bring the same level of familiarity to my teams. Work feels a lot less stressful when it involves a laid-back environment and transforms coworkers into friends.

The decision to either join Teach For America as a high school teacher or start at a more local middle school right out of college was a big one. My dream was to teach high school, but I wanted to stay close to home. Carolyn gave me the best advice: "Sometimes what you don't think you want is exactly what you need. And at the very least, you learn something about yourself." And thank God for her wisdom! My first years as a middle school teacher showed me how nurturing I am and introduced me to colleagues that are lifelong friends. I later followed my passion to teach high school, but those first three years made me the teacher I am today. Thank you, Carolyn. Next time we meet, I owe you some homemade muffins!

34

Listen to Feedback

Criticism is a part of any work environment (and relationship, but that's for another section!). Expecting to be perfect at anything, especially from the get-go, is unrealistic. Feedback is there to give you direction. As a manager and CEO, I promise you there's nothing wrong with making a mistake if you actively work to improve and grow from it. Get comfortable saying, "I made a mistake," and follow it up with, "I will work to do better."

Listen to the feedback and focus on the improvement you can make rather than defending yourself.

As a general manager, there was a manager under me who was responsible for a team of nine. She cried every time I tried to give her feedback. She would get so upset that she had to leave the room before I could finish and share how she could improve. Unfortunately, this happened so often it impeded our ability to work, and I had to take her out of the leadership role. I was frustrated that I couldn't help her grow professionally because she had a great deal of potential.

It's understandable to feel emotional when overwhelmed by feedback, but you must remain professional and save the tears for when you're alone. It's important your manager feels they can work with you and support you. The purpose of criticism is to hear it, reflect, and learn from it, which you cannot do if you take it personally.

When receiving feedback, take responsibility. Remain receptive and appreciative. If your boss critiques you, do not make excuses, even if it feels unfair in the moment. Reframe your thinking: your boss took the time to work with you and wouldn't give feedback if they weren't invested in your success. Remember, your accomplishments are a positive reflection of them, so they want you to do well. With that in mind, own your part! Even if you feel that a situation was completely out of your control, there is often some part you could have done differently. Listen to the feedback and focus on the improvement you can make rather than defending yourself.

There might be situations where your boss's feedback is unfounded. If you feel strongly this is the case, take time to reflect and digest it, and then discuss it with your boss. Be as specific as possible about why you disagree. Further, if you feel you are being targeted by biased or prejudiced feedback, discuss it with human resources to resolve the issue. Hopefully, you will never have to deal with an abuse of the workplace power dynamic and can simply use your feedback to grow.

When receiving criticism, follow these suggestions:

1. Ignore the volume; listen to the message.

Not all managers have great delivery. I strongly urge you to get beyond the noise and embrace the message. What is your boss really trying to say? What is the concern? Identify it, own it, and work at it. This will help you be a strong employee willing to grow.

2. Ask questions.

When receiving feedback, it's important that you ask questions so that you completely understand the critique. You can ask for an example for clarity. Just make sure your tone is inquisitive rather than skeptical or aggressive.

3. Seek advice.

I also recommend that you ask your boss for suggestions on how you can improve and grow your skills to avoid repeating the mistake. Write those suggestions down!

4. Follow up.

I advise that within twenty-four hours of meeting with your boss, send a follow-up email to thank them for their time, summarize your understanding of the critique, and list ways you will improve so that this won't be a concern moving forward. You can also ask if you missed anything or if they have any further suggestions.

5. Be proactive.

If you are proactive, you can sometimes avoid frequent feedback. If you need help developing a skill or you've made a mistake, reach out and ask for support. A good boss will appreciate the initiative and honesty.

Criticism is a part of everyone's career. The better you are at hearing it, digesting it, and using it wisely, the better you will be at your job.

COURTNEY COMMENT

What if the feedback is personal? I think women in the workplace run into this more than men. If we are too outspoken, we are insubordinate. If we care too much, we are emotional. if we "act like men," we are aggressive. Some of the best qualities women bring to the workplace end up critiqued.

It is hard! And I hear you. All marginalized groups, not just women, are more vulnerable to being mistreated in the workplace. I am sorry if you have ever been the target of such abuse.

What I will say is that if you find the right work environment, none of that will matter. You will be supported and celebrated for those traits. My dad is one of those bosses. They do exist.

If you feel the criticism is too personal or unfair and this is a consistent problem, you might have an HR issue or need to find a new garden in which to blossom.

If you're in a position of power and reading this, I ask that you actively support the equal treatment of marginalized groups in your workplace. It makes everyone better! Thank you.

35

Be an Eagle

There is a famous story attributed to author, businessman, and motivational speaker Harvey Mackay about eagles and ducks. He discusses a cab ride with a sharply dressed driver named Wally who gave him top-notch service: a sparkling car, a business card with a mission statement, an assortment of drinks including fresh coffee, a list of music stations, and asked whether he would prefer to learn about the sights or sit with his thoughts.

When Mackay asked Wally if he always gave such exceptional service, Wally said he had only begun to in recent years, after hearing personal growth guru Wayne Dyer discuss his book *You'll See It When You Believe It* on the radio. Apparently, Dyer said, "Stop complaining! Differentiate yourself from your competition. Don't be a duck. Be an eagle. Ducks quack and complain. Eagles soar above the crowd." This was the catalyst for Wally to reflect on his life and do better. Since then, he's happier, he's more satisfied, and his earnings have doubled!

"Don't be a duck. Be an eagle. Ducks quack and complain. Eagles soar above the crowd."

—HARVEY MCKAY

No matter the situation, ducks complain and deflect responsibility. Eagles, on the other hand, get the job done with a smile on their face in the midst of chaos. Eagles advance in their careers faster and further than most. Aim to be an eagle! No matter what the obstacle, task, or situation, find a way to rise above it.

I always notice the Wallys in the world and have even brought them into my business from other careers. When given an opportunity, they never cease to amaze me. I found one such eagle working at a local men's boutique. I admired his general aptitude for customer service and how he put people at ease. I gave him a chance, and he became a strong recruiter. I have also hired someone who waited on me at a restaurant and someone else who was a college coach. They are people who I saw remaining calm in stressful situations, hustling, and taking pride in their work. Eagles, with training, can be successful anywhere.

I recently spoke with a chief sales officer for one of the largest technology companies. He shared that when he looked to bring in more women, he brought together his best female staff, his eagles, to brainstorm where he could find more workers like them. They all had friends to recommend, most of whom worked retail. What happened? He hired them, and they were eagles, too. Why does retail have so many eagles? They work weekends, evenings, crazy hours, and are often unappreciated and earning little money. If they can hustle and smile through that, when given a chance at a different career path, they soar.

No matter what you do, I challenge you to avoid complaining with the ducks and channel that inner eagle in the most difficult of times. If you do, you will always have a career full of opportunities.

COURTNEY COMMENT

I like to consider myself an eagle, and I have my parents to thank for this work ethic and mentality. That doesn't mean it's always healthy for me.

I will never forget when I lived at home during my first year of teaching. One night, my parents sat me down when I arrived back from work after a fifteen-hour day, which was becoming a common habit, to share their concerns.

They legitimately thought I was manic. Looking back, maybe they were right. My students didn't have time to complete filling out the headings in their notebooks, so rather than wait and have them finish the next day, I stayed at work to complete all fifty myself. I spent sleepless nights making individual whiteboards for each student, grading more than students even cared to review, and creating PowerPoints that we never got through.

I did many amazing and non-crazy things, too, but I think my extreme behaviors raise an important point: eagles need boundaries and balance. If you consider yourself an eagle as well, remember, it's okay, even necessary, to take breaks. Skip lunch here or there, but don't let it become a habit.

I have worked in therapy to tone down the "eagleness," and I am now much happier. Guess what? I'm still a great teacher even without my handmade whiteboards!

36

The Show Must Go On

At the start of each workday, I prepare myself for five unexpected things to happen. Yes, I hear the irony—I prepare to be unprepared. But it works! Although any number of unanticipated things can happen in any given moment, I can control how I react to them. I put my energy there rather than fixate on the aggravation. Change is the only constant in the workplace, so always being ready to overcome obstacles will help you succeed professionally.

There might be an unplanned fire drill during your ten AM call, or a customer service problem that demands you clear your calendar. The possibilities are endless, and they are frustrating. But the show must go on! Schedules can shift. Plans may change. React, adjust, and keep moving forward. I suggest addressing any issues that arise before the day's end, put a plan in place, and start fresh the next morning. Again, problems will always occur; how you respond to them will tell others a lot about who you are as a professional. Embracing the unexpected with positivity, flexibility, and resourcefulness will make you indispensable (and keep you sane).

You must react, adjust, and keep moving forward.

I once ran a workshop for over five hundred people in Atlanta. I flew in from Philadelphia the night before, but my luggage never made it. The airport staff assured me there was nothing to worry about and that they would locate my luggage and bring it to the hotel later that night. Eight PM—still no luggage. I called the airport again, and they promised me they would find it and get it there in the middle of the night. I woke up at three in the morning frantic with no suitcase waiting. It was the early 2000s and everyone wore suits to these events. Mine were in that bag. Worse, I threw my daily contacts out before bed and would be blind!

Morning came, and it was clear my luggage wasn't coming. It was out of my control, and it was time to adjust and move forward. Professionals traveled and paid for top-notch training, and I had to deliver. I quickly purchased toiletries, but a suit and contacts would take longer. So, on day one, blind as an underdressed bat, I got up in front of hundreds of well-dressed professionals in sweats and a t-shirt and opened with an apology. I joked that if anyone raises a hand and I ignore them, it's not because I don't like them. I just can't see! I shared the story of the missing luggage, and everyone had a good laugh. My bag never did show up, but Michele found contacts and purchased business attire for the rest of the week. It was stressful, but humor and a positive attitude carried me through. For you, it might be resourcefulness and ingenuity. Handle your five unexpected things with integrity, even in the most trying of situations, so the show can go on!

COURTNEY COMMENT

My dad's story is part of a recurring nightmare I have. I dream that I'm unable to see clearly. I'm disoriented and scared, everything is blurry, and I can't make out details (psychoanalyze that!). My dad lived this bad dream and made it a success. Once again, the legend in action!

I'm sure you have your fair share of stories like my dad's. Life happens. Teaching is flooded with these moments! We are experts at handling the unexpected, and it's estimated we make 1,500 decisions a day, or four a minute, so we are constantly putting out fires and adapting.[1]

---

[1] Busy Teacher Admin, "Teachers—The Real Masters of Multitasking," Busy Teacher, https://busyteacher.org/16670-teachers-masters-of-multitasking-infographic.html. Last accessed July 30, 2021.

I will never forget when I was being observed by one of my supervisors during a lesson and the Wi-Fi went out. My entire lesson was on the computer and involved students working from their own devices. After sixty seconds of continuously trying to reconnect, I realized the plane was spiraling toward the ground, and I needed my parachute, stat.

What did I do? I told the students to put their Chromebooks in their bags, grab a notebook, and pull their desks into a circle. The lesson was supposed to be a thesis writing activity, so I used funny debates (think: the chicken or the egg) and had students write their arguments down, rip them out, throw them in the center, and then go pick up someone else's to review and defend. It was fabulous! The show went on, and it was the most engaged that class had been in months.

As much as we like to be prepared, life throws curveballs. I am starting to learn the more I accept them, the easier life is. If you're Type A like me, you'll understand what an undertaking this is.

I encourage you to swing at those curveballs! Find a way. You might even surprise yourself and hit a homerun. Or you might strike out, and in that case, just blame it on the lost contacts.

37

Manage Your Manager

Amanager's role is to help you understand your responsibilities and facilitate your growth so you can deliver the best results. Establishing a strong working relationship with your boss is essential to your career, and doing so will help you avoid common workplace issues. The following tips will help you navigate and establish this vital relationship.

1. Identify how you're evaluated.

Your boss will not see everything that you do, but if you know their priorities, you can make sure they see your most goal-aligned accomplishments. If your boss cares most about collaboration, regularly share how you are supporting and working with your colleagues. If innovation is most important to them, share your use of new technology. Many jobs have specific evaluation models or methods. Know the measure used in addition to your boss's expectations, and check in regularly since things can change.

When I was bartending, I worked under two owners. One owner was older, and he put his kids through college with the bar business. He cared about the numbers. When I spoke with him, I focused on revenue. I knew how each register performed and explained why one register might be slower than the others. The other owner was young and cared more about entertainment. With him, I discussed theme nights, bands, and signature drinks. It's an important skill to be able to adjust to your manager's preferences.

2. Understand communication and leadership styles.

Managers are people too, and they have unique communication and leadership styles. If you understand who you're working for, you can work together more effectively. If your boss prefers the phone to email, for example, give them a call to connect. Understand their preferences and personalities, and act accordingly.

I once had a boss whose leadership style was to micromanage. He would call my direct reports constantly and check up on them rather than going through me. I wanted the chance to manage my people, but meeting my boss with anger would not magically make him trust me. He was clearly uncomfortable giving me control and wanted to know every detail of the operation. I promised to update him daily if he allowed me to be the contact for my salespeople. I left him a voice-mail every night explaining what each person had accomplished, and the problem was solved. Understanding your boss's style will help you navigate issues.

3. Honor their time.

Your manager has many responsibilities, and you're probably not their only direct report. Respecting their time and energy is important. Do not bombard them with questions or unnecessarily stretch out meetings. If you need more support, ask them if they could schedule a meeting for thirty minutes at their convenience, and honor the half hour. Come prepared with specific questions and prioritize what you wish to discuss.

4. Respect the chain of command.

Every business has a chain of command you should follow. Respecting your boss means following this chain and never bypassing them. If you think you need to go above your boss to have a problem solved, resist that urge. The higher-ups won't appreciate it, and you will alienate your boss. You must work within a system to thrive.

I also recommend letting your manager know your moves before others. For example, if you will be taking a leave or asking to switch departments, let your boss know first.

5. Perform well.

If your job performance is above average, your manager will trust you more and worry less. Essentially, the better you perform, the easier you make their job and yours. I suggest you under-promise and over-deliver so that you are always exceeding expectations.

It is also helpful to understand and avoid your boss's triggers. For example, my first manager focused on expense report deadlines. If yours was late, you were on the chopping block, so mine were always early at the expense of anything else. Do your best to prioritize what your boss prioritizes.

6. Help them achieve their goals.

How is your manager being evaluated? If you understand how your boss's success is measured, you can support them in those goals. Your manager will appreciate you helping them advance their agendas. In return, they will often give you more trust, respect, and acknowledgment.

7. Establish a personal connection.

Not all bosses want a friendly relationship, but you can work on making a personal connection. If your manager likes you, they're more willing to work with you. When I was sixteen and working at McDonalds, I went out of my way to be friendly with my boss. He was passionate about sports and graduated from Hofstra, so I discussed these topics with him to form a connection. When I started to struggle with the work schedule because the two buses I took did not run on weekends, he was happy to schedule me for weeknights instead.

Managers are people too, and they have unique communication and leadership styles.

---

8. Follow up in writing.

Like you, your boss is juggling a lot of balls. It is always wise to follow up meetings with an email to summarize your takeaways and next steps. This allows you to document what you discussed for reference and to check for understanding.

9. Refrain from gossip.

It is tempting to vent about your boss and succumb to watercooler gossip. Resist! Give your manager the benefit of the doubt. You never know when your words will get back to them and reflect negatively. Do not jeopardize this most-important relationship. Stay professional.

10. Share your long-term goals.

Your boss is not a mind-reader. You can achieve your professional goals if you share them. When the time is appropriate, communicate your long-term goals with your manager so they can advocate for you if an opportunity arises.

There are plenty of kind, mean, successful, unsuccessful, funny, stern, realistic, and unrealistic bosses out there. You cannot control who your boss is (although you can choose to leave if you are in a toxic situation). No matter who your manager is, follow these tips and you'll have a better chance at a productive working relationship. It's okay to manage your manager.

COURTNEY COMMENT

Your boss can be your strongest advocate when you foster the relationship.

One of my career goals was to teach in a high school setting; however, my first three years were at a middle school. My manager understood my desire to work with teens since I openly shared this with her. She also respected my work because I met her goals and expectations.

As a result, when it came time to request a transfer, she guided me through the process and supported this move within the district. Essentially, she helped make it happen!

I strongly urge you to share your long-term goals with your manager and let them support your growth. Remember, climbing the ladder is much easier if you have help along the way. Ask for it. Cultivate it. And welcome it.

38

Present and Implement Solutions

Anyone can complain about problems, but it's the person who offers solutions that's invaluable.

When approaching your boss with an issue, always bring a solution with a clear implementation plan. Thomas Edison perceptively explained, "Vision without execution is hallucination." Discussing ideas can be helpful, but it's the actual execution of them that brings real progress. I recommend you present a solution that doesn't create more work for your boss and that you volunteer to take charge. This demonstrates vision and leadership.

"Vision without execution is hallucination."

—THOMAS EDISON

One of the most frustrating parts of my job selling shipping equipment at Alcatel was that our inefficient customer service often lost new clients (and my hard-earned sales) before their payment was due. When I captured a client, they signed a purchase agreement and we shipped out the product immediately, not collecting payment for thirty days. The shipping equipment had a learning curve and sometimes needed repairs. In those scenarios, a call to our service department always ruined the deal—it took two to three days for our customer service to get out to the client and solve the issue (our competitor had them up and running the same day).

The solution? I asked my boss if I could collect a 10% deposit when a new client signed a purchase agreement. They would be less likely to cancel the deal in those first thirty days if they had money invested, and it gave us time to fix the problems. I also worked with the service department and helped them update their system to prioritize new clients. It changed everything. I was promoted shortly after, and I believe this was the reason. It is this type of initiative and solution-based approach to your job that will help you advance faster and win the respect of your higher-ups as well.

COURTNEY COMMENT

A common student critique I hear is that the workload in my class is unrealistic. When students bring this to my attention, I commiserate with them and also suggest they use class time more efficiently. They then like to remind me that the less work I assign, the less I need to grade. Touché, young buck, touché. But also unrealistic—they need opportunities and feedback to grow.

One time, this complaint came with a clear and easy solution. A student suggested we take the first ten minutes of class on Fridays to begin homework and address questions. She also recommended extending due dates to Mondays to give them more time to work. This required minimal effort on my part. The student reminded me to take ten on Fridays and adjust deadlines when I forgot. A win-win!

No matter the scenario, you'll achieve more victories if you approach your boss with a solutions-based mindset that puts the responsibility of execution on you.

39

Be a Team Player

Aworkplace's climate and culture are greatly influenced by its people. Yes, leadership can have a major impact on company culture by appreciating staff, encouraging creativity, and listening with follow-up. However, the day-to-day environment is largely fueled by YOU!

When you're collaborative, you create an environment where people build each other up, and everyone is better for it.

How can you be a positive influence? Be a team player. Collaborating with your colleagues promotes a supportive environment as well as innovation. I will never forget when my then coworker and now good friend Scott Rachman helped me make my first sale at Alcatel. I was nervous about doing the demonstration because it was on an incredibly complicated piece of shipping equipment. I asked Scott if he would help me present it to the potential client. Although he was busy, he said he would try to stop by. I started the presentation, and Scott was nowhere in sight. As I feared, I was struggling—the shipping scales weren't working.

Suddenly, as if appearing from the heavens, Scott walked in and saved me. Everything fell into place. There was nothing in it for him (although he still reminds me that I owe him!), but I made my first big sale. That act of kindness gave us an instant connection, and it inspired me to always try to pay it forward and help others.

At Alcatel, I helped my colleagues just as Scott had helped me. When I was first promoted (over people with much more experience), my boss told me it was because my coworkers shared that I helped them even when it wasn't my responsibility. Being a team player was something I believed in, and it also helped me get promoted. More importantly, it made the workplace safe and enjoyable.

When you're collaborative, you create an environment where people build each other up, and everyone is better for it. You want to go to work when surrounded by positive, likeminded people. The opposite can also be true. If you work with people who are negative and cutthroat, you might avoid the workplace altogether. If you cannot trust or laugh with the people around you, you miss crucial opportunities to learn from one another. It's important to avoid negative watercooler talk. It's easy to get sucked in. Be able to defend your company or leave it.

It only takes one person to improve a work environment, and that person can be you. Be the catalyst for positive change in your office. Help a coworker who is struggling. Bring in a card for a birthday celebration. Compliment your boss. Share something you learned. You will see how infectious this type of behavior is and how it transforms your job.

COURTNEY COMMENT

There is nothing more demoralizing than a negative teacher's lounge. Okay, I'm hyperbolizing. I'm sure the waiting room at the endodontist is pretty miserable.

When I was student teaching, my mentor told me her best piece of advice was to stay out of the faculty lounge. I'm a major people person, so this was difficult! How can I learn from my peers if I avoid gathering with them? I found that her recommendation is sometimes true, but not always (although it was true for her school).

It all depends on where you work. I was at one school where the teacher's lounge was uplifting: goodies baked for each other, pictures on the walls, and fun stories shared about our beloved students. I always went there for encouragement, ideas, and positive vibes. On the flipside, I student taught somewhere else with a teacher's lounge that could not be more different: grunting about bosses, drab walls, and sauce stains on the sofa. Dissatisfaction filled the air, and the longer you stayed, the more it crept under your skin. It became a place I avoided altogether.

Does that mean we have to accept the culture of our workplace and respond accordingly by either joining in or avoiding office interactions? Not at all. Sure, ambiance affects you, but like my dad said, you can also affect it.

When I worked at my current district's middle school, I joined a grade level team full of many different and amazing personalities. There were eight of us, but there was little collaboration because our classrooms were physically distant. As an eager new hire, I baked cupcakes for the first birthday of the year and brought them to a meeting. This group of previously quiet teachers instantly lit up and stayed after to enjoy the treat over lunch. We were laughing, discussing our families and favorite TV shows, and swapping tips for opening day. This became a tradition for each birthday, and we became a close group that supported each other and shared ideas. A little personal touch goes a long way, and often people are just waiting for a chance at connection!

40

Cultivate Success Working from Home

Working remote, or remotely working? Working from home gets a bad rap. Images of people in pajamas eating potato chips with the TV blasting come to mind. But working from home is widely expanding, especially in a post-pandemic world, and the data stands in contrast to those images.

Turnover is 50% less for remote workers than in-person employees, and a Stanford study found that remote employees produced one full day's work more a week than their in-office counterparts.[2] Hiring remote broadens the candidate pool and reduces cost. For many companies, it's a no-brainer and the way of the future.

Working from home...requires a lot of discipline.

---

[2] Nicholas Bloom, James Liang, John Roberts, and Zhichun Jenny Ying, "Does Working from Home Work? Evidence from a Chinese Experiment," *The Quarterly Journal of Economics* 130 no. 1, November 20, 2014, https://academic.oup.com/qje/article-abstract/130/1/165/2337855?redirectedFrom=fulltext. Last accessed July 30, 2021.

As an employee, working from home eliminates a commute, increases autonomy, and reduces business interruptions. Many people feel it creates more work-life balance, and they enjoy the flexibility and independence. If these advantages sound appealing to you, it might be time to pursue a job with work-from-home capability.

But, beware! Working from home is also incredibly difficult and requires a lot of discipline. Will household chores get in the way of your productivity? Will your family or housemates respect your space? Will the phone and TV impede efficiency? Will you be able to truly disconnect after work if the job always sits a room away? There is a lot to consider, but the following tips will help you be successful when working remote.

1. Set Boundaries.

Working from home is an opportunity to cultivate more work-life balance. Unfortunately, the opposite can occur, and you either work all the time or not enough. To be successful, you must create boundaries around your work and personal hours. This might mean telling your partner that they cannot come in when you are on calls. Or that your children must respect your privacy when the door is shut. It's hard to do when the dog is barking and the baby is crying, but you must protect working hours to remain productive. The same goes for your personal time. If an email comes in at 7 PM asking you to update a data sheet while you're eating dinner with your significant other or putting your son to bed, you have to ignore it. It might feel quick and easy to go into the office for five minutes, but it's not fair to your loved ones (and it's never only five minutes). When you no longer have a commute to transition from work to home, you must be more intentional at protecting your "you" time.

2. Check-in with work often.

Because you don't see your colleagues daily, it's possible to land on different pages in a remote environment. To avoid doing unnecessary or duplicate work, connect with your teammates and boss daily. Share what you're working on, ask questions, and support each other regardless of your physical location. It's easy to go a week without talking to a colleague when you don't see anyone in person, but don't let this happen! Staying connected will also mitigate feelings of isolation.

3. Cultivate a presence.

Although you're not in a physical office space, cultivating a presence within your company is essential to getting recognition, raises, and promotions. Embrace in-person gatherings, join company retreats, attend the office holiday party, and physically show up for important meetings. Make a personal connection, and don't allow yourself to be overlooked.

Remote relationship building takes some creativity. Instead of bringing someone a coffee, consider buying them one by sending a five-dollar Starbucks gift card. Mail cards rather than leaving a post-it note or card on someone's desk. Send a coworker a message to lend an ear if you know they're going through a tough time. Organize a birthday call to celebrate a colleague's big day. There are many opportunities to build relationships, even when working from home.

4. Clarify expectations.

Since you're not receiving live feedback working from home, it's important to ensure you completely understand what's expected of you. You will not be able to see your boss's face when reviewing work or read the social cues when presenting a finding. You won't be able to walk over and ask a quick question. This makes clear guidelines even more important! Otherwise, you might waste a day working on something that needs to be re-done.

5. Know the technology.

Working remote is easier when you embrace all the technological resources available, and those are endless. Video conferencing is crucial. Make sure you are competent at your company's platform of choice. Be able to set meetings using the company's digital calendar, and work on efficient digital communication. It's important to learn how to create presentations and screen share to present data from home to a group. This will make your remote position more feasible and your ability to do it unquestionable.

6. Invest in the culture.

It can be difficult to feel company culture from home, but it's not impossible. Many companies will hold digital happy hours, companywide calls, and traditions such as Monday morning coffee. Join in these events. Companies usually have unspoken ways of communicating digitally, and I recommend embracing that part of the culture as well. Communicate the way your boss does, whether that is creating a bitmoji or using memes.

7. Meet deadlines.

The worst mistake you can make when working remote is missing a deadline. It is even more detrimental when working from home than in the office because your boss cannot see the time that you have (or have not) been putting in: if your work is subpar or late, the assumption will be that you were not focused or working enough hours.

8. Communicate. And then communicate some more.

When you do not see your colleagues in person, it's easy to misunderstand each other. Realize that people might communicate differently over email or text; you might need to hop on a call to clarify comments or concerns. Do not be impulsive or reactive when receiving written communication. Rather, be clear, forgiving, and in constant contact. Working remote is like being in a long-distance relationship, and you must put in the effort to make it work.

9. Follow a schedule and practice self-discipline.

It is easy to waste time when working remote. In an actual office, you are redirected by external cues such as a coworker asking a question or your boss walking past your cubicle. At home, you don't have these same cues. I suggest following a schedule. Have a specific time you sign on. Schedule breaks (make sure you break to eat, get outside, and interact with others). Resist the distractions, and stay disciplined so you can stick to your schedule and reach your goals.

10. Always be professional.

I recommend, if needed, you get dressed professionally every day. People who dress the part are often more productive. Sweats make us feel tired. However, if you do wear your pajamas to work from home, make sure you put on business clothes for video. It is easy to get too comfortable when working in your own space, but it is essential that you remember you are part of a work environment. This means you must present professionally, speak respectfully, dress and act conservatively, and keep your personal problems private.

Working remote has many advantages, but for it to be viable for your career, it is important to embrace these tips. After all, if working remote becomes remotely working, you might lose the option to work from home entirely. Or even worse, you could end up losing your job. With a little intention and a lot of discipline, you can make a remote job right for both you and your company.

COURTNEY COMMENT

Make sure you have separate video conferencing accounts for your personal and professional lives. You do not want to log on to a company meeting with the username "Sexy Thang" on your screen (hey, tipsy happy hours with your friends get goofy). Don't become the next viral YouTube video.

At the beginning of the COVID-19 pandemic, my sister had a Zoom call with her college friends and jokingly changed her background to a shirtless man. A few days later, her son was using Zoom with his first-grade class. He was using her account...with the same shirtless man! She had forgotten to change the background. Luckily, she switched it quickly, but his teacher still saw and had a good laugh.

This is why separate accounts are critical!

41

Strive for Work-Life Balance

When I look at American society, the lack of balance makes me incredibly sad. Beginning with babies all the way up to adults, we pack our schedules to the brim with music classes, endless hours of homework, and midnight Door Dash deliveries on the company dime (as a ploy to get employees to work late). Long gone are the days of endless Capture the Flag in the neighbor's backyard and the family dinners without interruption.

What is the result of this new way of life? I strongly believe our inability to manage work boundaries plays a major role in the decline of physical and mental health in our country. America is one of the most anxious and depressed, as well as physically unhealthy, countries in the world. Is this a necessary evil in the quest for success?

I don't believe so. I would even argue that the more balance you find, the more successful you'll be. The more time I spend on myself, the better my company performs. I began in corporate America where my average day was fourteen hours, leaving little time for my family or personal pursuits. I left for work when my kids were still asleep and arrived home when they were already tucked in; I missed so many firsts, from first steps to first days of school. Though I was providing for my family and moving up the corporate ladder, my physical and mental health were suffering. I resented the trade-offs, which ultimately affected my work potential.

You can have it all.

When I set boundaries to regain work-life synergy, I was initially concerned that I might jeopardize my boss's positive impression of me, seeing me as lazy or undedicated rather than a dependable overachiever. However, this never happened because I was still able to meet all my work goals. In fact, both my professional and personal lives improved drastically as a result, and it helped me be more positive at work.

How can you put similar habits in place?

1. Focus more while at work; work smarter not harder.
2. Shut down all devices at home.
3. Schedule daily time for yourself and your family.
4. Sleep well.
5. Exercise.
6. Eat healthy.
7. Maintain friendships.

I found that if I prioritized what I valued most, I was happier and more successful at my job. This meant I would miss fewer "firsts": I would rearrange my schedule to make it to the band concert or go in earlier to make it home for dinner.

I acknowledge this is not an easy task in a culture that rewards long hours and companies that pay your phone bill so you can access email twenty-four seven. Realistically, there are points in your career where you will have to pay your dues and work overtime; however, if this is a regular occurrence, you will resent it.

If you find a company whose culture embraces balance, you'll thrive. As an executive recruiter, I know there are companies that have policies that support and encourage work-life harmony. Once offered a job, I encourage you to inquire about:

- Parental leave policies
- Sick days
- Paid vacation time
- Guidelines for working hours
- Perks such as gym memberships

These policies will let you know if a company is invested in you as a person as well as an employee.

Sometimes, prioritizing yourself means letting go of your dreams of mansions and Maseratis. Other times, prioritizing yourself is exactly what you need to achieve it. Either way, this new mindset will lead to a happier, healthier you. You can have it all.

COURTNEY COMMENT

In my first years of teaching, I was often the last to leave work and would proudly post a picture to my social media accounts of my lonely little car illuminated by the lamplight. I wanted to showcase what I thought was a healthy work ethic. But what was I actually showing off? The fact that I had no life outside the school's four walls? Is that really what I want to be proud of?

At the end of the day, I wasn't the best teacher. I was not the best daughter or friend. Putting in the most time did not equate to happiness or success. So, I found ways to work smarter. I started timing how long my lesson plans took, setting goals to decrease it each week. When I began to be able to go to yoga again and out on a date, I felt better and more fulfilled. Most importantly, that's when I became a better teacher.

You can be successful without losing everything that matters to you. And now that I have a son, I better not be that last lone car in the lot ever again.

PART FOUR

PERSONAL FINANCE

42

Living on Your Own:
A Monthly Budget

Over the years, the "Moving Out" session with my interns has always been one of the most important ones. I sit down with these intelligent college students and ask how many of them want to move out of their childhood homes after graduation. Almost all of them emphatically respond, "Yes!" Then I ask the follow-up question: "Do you know what it will cost?" and I am met with blank stares or misguided guesses.

**Establishing independence is a part of growing up
and starting your own life.**

Establishing independence is a part of growing up and starting your own life. The following chart outlines the expenses to consider when budgeting for the cost of living on your own. Your personal situation will greatly impact the number you budget in each category. This chart will help you think through each expense and how much money you'll need to afford this milestone.

Monthly Expenses

EXPENSE	CONSIDERATIONS	BUDGET
Rent	–Where? –Alone or with roommates? –Amenities?	–Anywhere from $400–$2,000/month –You should spend no more than 30% of your gross (pre-tax) income on rent and utilities combined
Utilities	–Electric –Gas –Water/Sewer* –Security* –Trash* –Internet/Cable/Phone (*Frequently included in rent)	–Use a utility cost calculator by zip code to estimate (about $250/month in an apartment, and more in a house) –Varies each month depending upon usage and season –Ask for average cost of utilities before signing a lease
Renter's or Homeowner's Insurance	–Shop it to get the best price –Use a reputable company	–Renter's: usually less than $200/year –Homeowner's: around $1,500/year; can vary greatly
Food	–Will you cook? Eat out? –Where do you grocery shop?	–About 11% of take-home income (average $150–$300/month)
Cell Phone	–How much data? –Family plan? –Best service in your area? –Type of phone?	–About $75–$150/month *Also consider the cost of the phone itself
Medical, Dental, and Vision Insurance	–Employee coverage or private plan? –Copay? –Regular appointments? –Need vision coverage? –FSA or HSA? –Level of coverage?	–About $375/month for an individual plan through employer at age twenty-one –Usually, companies pay part and deduct the rest from your paycheck –Can stay on parent/guardian's plan until age twenty-six
Transportation	–Need public transportation? –Parking? Gas? Car insurance?	Situational: –Walk to work? $0 –Car in the city? $600/month in some places

EXPENSE	CONSIDERATIONS	BUDGET
Loans	–Debt? –Monthly college loan payment? –Monthly credit card payment?	Situational: –Average college loan payment is about $400/month
Savings	–401(k) contribution? –Personal savings for a "rainy day?" *A rainy-day fund, or emergency fund, is an amount of money set aside to cover three to six months of expenses. This is what you would use in a crisis such as loss of work, an unexpected home repair, or medical expenses.	–Optional, but recommended about 20% of gross income
Entertainment	–What do you do for fun and what are the associated costs? –Think concerts, parties, vacations, videogames, movies	–Budget about 5% of your gross income
Miscellaneous	–Cable upgrade –Clothing/other shopping –Gifts –Repairs and other one-offs	–Budget about 5% of your gross income

The sum of the column on the right is the cost of living independently. So, what salary do you need to accomplish this goal? Since you only take home about two-thirds of that salary after taxes, increase your total by 30% to see the actual income you must earn to support your lifestyle. Upon completion of this exercise, my interns' eyes are usually bulging.

There's a lot to consider when moving out. Living independently is difficult, but with planning, it is very possible. If you get nothing else from this exercise, I hope at the very least you will give your parents or guardians a great big hug because they have been paying for all this!

COURTNEY COMMENT

Why does adulting have to be so hard?!

I had a friend who immediately moved into an apartment after graduation. When he received his first paycheck, he realized he couldn't afford his rent because his take home pay was much less after deductions. He was eventually evicted.

This doesn't have to be you!

Make an informed budget and follow it. I find the budgeting process to be therapeutic. I feel in control of my life, and we Type A people love that feeling. More laid-back? You can still find painless ways to keep your spending on track.

I initially used an app on my phone called **Best Budget** to track my spending. I could create my own budget categories, and I liked their charts and the ease of inputting data in real time from my device. My husband and I now use **Google Sheets** to track our monthly budget since we can easily share data, use formulas, and format entries. Find a method that works for you!

43

College Loans

Higher education in the United States has become just that—higher and higher in cost. Forbes reported that U.S. college loan debt reached almost 1.6 trillion dollars in 2020, and the average college graduate owes $20,000 to $35,000. The average total price for a four-year degree is about $122,000 at a public university and almost $200,000 at a private institution.[1]

**The average loan takes twenty years to pay off
and you can feel like a prisoner to that payment.**

Student loan debt can follow you for a quarter of a century and delay your ability to move out on your own, get married, or even afford a dinner out at a restaurant. It can be incredibly difficult to get out from under it. How did we get here?

I strongly believe that the student debt problem in our country stems from a belief that to be successful you must attend the best four-year

---

[1] Melanie Hanson, "Student Loan Debt Statistics," Educationdata.org, last modified July 10, 2020, https://educationdata.org/student-loan-debt-statistics. Last accessed July 30, 2021.

college to which you are accepted. This has become part of the American Dream and is the mentality that gets so many people into financial trouble.

My friend's son Louis is a perfect example. My friend and his wife thought they were giving the best advice when they dissuaded him from going to the local community college for his first two years. They believed their son would have more opportunities going to a four-year institution. To do so, he commuted over an hour back and forth for classes, did not have the typical college experience, worked many jobs, and took out two different loans to cover his four years.

Fast forward to 2020 and Louis is thirty years old, living at home, and unable to marry his girlfriend of many years. He graduated owing almost $120,000 and pays about $1,000 a month in student loans. At the ten-year mark, one loan will be paid off and then he'll pay about $600 a month for ten more years. If he could do it all over again, he would make very different choices.

There are many ways to avoid Louis's situation.

1. Two Years of Community College

The best way to save money on college while still obtaining a degree from a reputable institution is by attending a community college for the first two years of your studies and then finishing at a four-year college. If you transfer to complete your bachelor's degree, your diploma will reflect only the school to which you transferred. On your resume, you only need to list the four-year university.

The perks? For the first two years of your post-secondary education, you can live at home to save money, and the courses are a fraction of the cost. You complete your introductory level courses there, and by the time you transfer, you are ready and more prepared to jump into your major. Your college debt will be half as much when you graduate and there is no harm done to your job potential. This is the exact route my son-in-law took to get his accounting degree, and his first job after college was at Deloitte. His minimal loans were paid off quickly.

2. Know Your End Goal

Before you invest in a college loan, know your end goal. Have you done the research to know your job potential when you finish your degree?

Do you know what salary you will make in that job? Will you be able to obtain work and start paying off your loans?

I am not suggesting that medical or law school is a bad decision. It may be expensive, but there is a job at the end, and you will eventually be able to pay off those loans. Most importantly, follow your dreams—just make sure they don't turn into a financial nightmare.

Wondering what the average starting salary is for your major? Check out this 2021 chart from the U.S. Census Bureau, American Community Survey summarizing unemployment rates and salary averages for graduates by field of study: https://www.newyorkfed.org/research/college-labor-market/college-labor-market_compare-majors.html

3. Find the Best Loan

Most college loans give graduates a six-month grace period before collecting. Then, you make payments monthly. Before taking out a loan, make sure you understand the type of loan, the interest rate, the loan term, associated fees, bonuses, options, and possible penalties. I suggest you do more research on these details before choosing the best loan for you.

4. When All Else Fails, Dig Yourself Out of The Hole

If you are already in the hole and making large monthly payments toward college debt, you are not alone. According to the Department of Education, the average loan takes twenty years to pay off, and you can feel like a prisoner to that payment. There are ways to lighten the load. Explore:

- Student loan forgiveness programs
- Income-based repayment plans
- Employer-based payment plans
- Second jobs (side hustles, as my children call them)

The more educated you are about your loans and your options, the better the situation.

COURTNEY COMMENT

As the wife of the son-in-law who went to community college and then transferred, I am incredibly grateful! My husband paid off his loans at the start of our marriage, allowing us to start saving sooner.

I took for granted the toll of higher education's price tag until I married Rich. I come from an affluent family who was able to pay for my degrees, which I know is not the norm for most people in our country. Understanding the cost of education changed my perspective on it greatly. Higher education isn't the only respectable choice!

I tell my students all the time that college is not the only path there is to take after high school. Joining the military, getting an apprenticeship, or taking a gap year to earn some money are all smart decisions that don't require taking on debt. But if you do choose the college route, my dad's tips will help you do so wisely.

44

Your Credit Score

Your credit score is a lot like your cholesterol: by the time you realize how bad it is, it takes a lot of work to get it back on track.

A common misconception about credit scores is that if you've never made any financial mistakes, you have good credit. That's just not true.

Take the case of my daughter-in-law: Olivia came out of graduate school with no debt, plenty of money in her savings account, and a great job. She needed financing to buy her first car. No problem, right? Wrong. Every dealership in town turned her down because she had no credit history.

Sure, she had chances to build credit while in college, but she didn't realize that was important. Her apartment was not in her name, she wasn't responsible for any of the utility bills, her current car was in her father's name, she wasn't on a cable bill, and she had a debit card, no credit card.

**Scores are fluid and directly correlate
with your financial activity.**

Her roommates who had these bills in their names were establishing credit. She paid them monthly for her share, but her credit history remained nonexistent. **The reality is that you need to borrow money and pay it back on time to have a high credit score.** Establishing credit is as simple as that, yet few young people know how to do this. You must actively build credit to have a score, and work to keep that score favorable.

Want to buy a house? You need a good credit score. Want to open a credit card? Lease a car? Start a business? Your credit score determines your ability to do so. A good credit score means you can get a loan, and the specific score dictates your interest rate, or fee, for the loan. The better the score, the lower the rate. Your credit score can also impact your insurance premium.

Your credit score is a number that represents you as a borrower and signifies to lenders how likely you are to repay the loan with interest. The three big credit bureaus (Transunion, Equifax, and Experian) calculate your score, and each gives you a slightly different number. You can get a free copy of your score from several sources, such as banks, credit cards, Credit Karma, and Credit Sesame. To calculate your score, referred to as your FICO or credit score, the credit bureaus review the information listed in the chart on the opposite page:

How Your Credit Score is Determined[2]

Category	% of credit score	Definition	What raises your score?	What lowers your score?
Credit History	35%	Past debt and how effectively you paid it back	–Paying all your bills on time –Never missing a payment	–Not paying bills on time –Missing a payment
Debt	30%	Current debt (credit card debt, student loans, car loan, mortgage)	–Your debt is less than your income –Low balances –Loans close to being paid off	–Your debt is more than your income –High balances –Maxed out credit cards –Loans have little payment history
Length of Credit	15%	The time between when you started making payments and the present	–The longer, the better –You have had the same credit card(s) for years	–Credit history is less than two years –History of debt, but no history of paying off the debt
Diversity of Debt	10%	Various types of accounts (installment loans, home loans, bills, and credit cards)	–Different monthly bills, such as phone, rent, utilities	–Only one credit card that you put everything on –Only one bill/loan in your name
New Credit	10%	Recently opened accounts	–You've had the same accounts for a long time and pay them off	–Recently applying for two new credit cards –Regularly opening new credit cards and canceling older ones

---

[2] "How Your Credit Score Is Calculated," Wells Fargo. https://www.wellsfargo.com/financial-education/credit-management/calculate-credit-score/. Last accessed July 30, 2021.

Once this information is reviewed, you will receive a score between 300 and 850, which represents your likelihood to repay debt. The higher the number, the better the credit. Anything below 580 is considered problematic, while anything above 670 is considered fair. Further, if you are at or above 760, you will receive the best rates and opportunities. Review the last two columns of the chart to understand how to improve your score.

Concerned you have already done too much damage? No worries!

How do you start to build or rebuild credit?

- Check your credit score often and track changes
- Work to improve your score (beginning with paying bills on time)
- Fix mistakes as soon as possible

Did You Know...? A child can be listed as an authorized user, or secondary account holder, on a parent's credit card and build credit through the parent's account transactions. Help your children start building credit!

Luckily, scores are fluid and directly correlate with your financial activity. So, with a little bit of work and attention, both cholesterol and credit scores can improve.

COURTNEY COMMENT

I always hesitate to check my credit score for fear that my rating will take a hit.

Where did this myth come from? Who knows, but if you share this feeling, I promise you that we did our research—checking your own credit rating or getting pre-approval is considered a soft inquiry and will not hurt your score. However, frequent hard inquiries can hurt it. A hard inquiry is when you apply for a loan or credit card and the creditor requests to see your credit file.

Have no fear and monitor your rating. I suggest using a digital tool such as **NerdWallet** that regularly updates your score using a consistent measure. This way, you can stay on top of identity theft too.

45

Credit Cards

Credit cards can be tricky to navigate. They make shopping easy—no need to carry cash when you can shop online with the click of a button! Credit cards allow you to make purchases that you don't have money for in the moment. But is that financially savvy?

Credit card debt is a major concern in our country, and it is the second largest national debt after student loans. Credit card debt traps people in deep financial holes that become seemingly impossible to climb out of, and credit card companies are piranhas profiting from your inability to pay back what you borrow. The basis of their business is to bet that you will not be able to pay back money on time and ultimately owe them more than they lent you. These companies benefit from impulsivity and naiveté, and they often set up shop on college campuses, handing out applications to young students. They hope that young people will jump at the opportunity to have what they see as "free money" *now*. The problem? When *later* comes, interest has accrued, and they owe much more than they realized.

Remember, credit cards can ruin your credit, so be careful! When applying for a credit card, make sure you shop around for the best one. To qualify for the best ones, you must have strong credit, so your first credit card might not be the most favorable. Identify which cards you qualify for, check their APR (or annual percentage rate—the interest rate as paid over the year) and annual fees, and investigate their rewards programs. Then choose the best card for you.

Once you have a credit card, **it is in your best interest to use it only when you know you will be able to pay it back on time**. Make sure you know when your payments are due. If you accidentally miss a payment deadline, you can call the credit card company and they will often waive the late fee if it's the first time you've missed a payment. After that, you will be charged interest and owe more than you spent.

To avoid missing payments and accumulating late fees, set up your online account and consider automated bill pay to have monthly payments made on your behalf and on time, given you have the money in the bank to cover the balance. You can also call your credit card company and change the date that your bill is due each month. I recommend choosing the day that falls immediately after you receive your paycheck.

The more that you owe and the longer you have owed it, the greater the interest rate becomes, and your debt accrues. Credit card interest rates are usually the highest there are, so you want to pay off your credit card debt before anything else. Student loan interest rates and mortgage interest rates are much, much lower.

Credit card debt traps people in deep financial holes that become seemingly impossible to climb out of.

An example will best illustrate the cost of credit card debt. Let's say you have a $1,000 credit card bill. If the APR is 20% and you cannot pay your bill that month, you will be charged a late fee of around thirty dollars and accrue 1.67% interest (the APR/twelve months). As a result, the next month you will owe $1,046.70 instead of $1,000 if you charge nothing new to the card. If the APR and late fee remain the same and you still cannot pay your balance, you will owe $1,094.18 the next month. Same thing in the third month? You are now up to $1,142.45. A year later? That $1,000 is now about $1,558.82, over 55% in lost value.

When you do go to make a credit card payment, you will often be informed of the minimum payment. Never pay just the minimum if you have the money. If you only make the minimum payment instead of the total balance, you accrue interest. You always want to pay the total balance if you can.

Credit cards also give you credit limits. A credit limit is a maximum amount you can spend. You want to try and spend only 30% of the limit to stay in good credit standing. The closer you get to the credit limit, the more your credit score will be negatively impacted. Credit card companies hope that you will spend up to your limit, not be able to pay the balance, and then accrue a great deal of interest. This is where they make their money.

Unhappy with your credit card and its rates? You can call your credit card company and request that they lower your APR after a few months of responsible usage. One study showed that the credit card company lowered the rate 50% of the time people called to inquire. A call can only help!

Overall, avoid thinking of a credit card as easy money or a rainy-day fund to pay for what you can't afford. This mentality could end up ruining your financial standing and destroy your credit. Credit cards are amazing opportunities to build credit and benefit from rewards, but only if you can pay your balance each month. Avoid the credit card trap!

COURTNEY COMMENT

Want to take that trip to Mexico with your friends but don't have the money? Charging your credit card and worrying about paying it off later is tempting, but it is not the answer. Those shots of tequila on the beach might taste good in the moment, but just like that tan, the good vibes will fade and you'll be left with a cost too large to bear. Take that trip when you can afford it, and it will be that much sweeter.

46

Taxes

Taxes. You cringe when you hear the word, but do you actually know what they are, how much you pay, and how to pay them? Taxes are a reality, and it serves you to understand the ins and outs so that you can properly prepare and avoid owing a great deal of money to the government come April 15.

People often assess a starting salary based upon the number in their offer letter. Big mistake! You take home a fraction of that. A large percentage (about 30% give or take) goes to taxes. That makes a major difference when budgeting.

The average starting salary for a college graduate is about $50,000. After deducting 30% for taxes, only $35,000 is left. This difference affects where you can afford to live, what bills you can pay, and if you can save.

When you begin working, you start to pay taxes. You fill out a W-4 at the start of a new job to indicate the amount deducted from your paycheck to cover your tax payment. This amount varies depending upon your personal situation (marital status, family, and so forth).

Be aware of how taxes impact your take-home salary.

The sum of your regular paychecks will not amount to your total salary since each paycheck has taxes withdrawn. You should calculate the amount that will be deducted from each paycheck so that you can budget realistically for the month based upon your actual take-home pay. You can use an online paycheck and tax withholding calculator to do so. The IRS, ADP, and others have free calculators you can use.

Finally, you must file your taxes by April 15 in a normal year. You can do it yourself, pay a small fee to use a service such as TurboTax, or pay an accountant to file for you. Sometimes you owe more money and sometimes you are refunded money depending upon how close your deduction estimate was. You will know for certain once you complete your tax return.

Taxes are a part of life. Luckily, your job does the deductions for you, and, as mentioned above, you can use a service for filing. What is most important is to be aware of how taxes impact your take-home salary so you can budget realistically.

COURTNEY COMMENT

If you're like me and it's all a little too overwhelming, just marry a CPA. Thanks, Rich! (Just kidding—the only special someone you need is TurboTax).

I also want to share how deductions affected my take-home pay. My salary as a seventh-year teacher with a master's degree in a New Jersey public school was $69,820. This is A LOT of money. That would be $3,491 twice a month for ten months of the year.

What I actually took home? $2,018.58. That is about 42% deducted. Aside from my federal taxes, state taxes, and FICA, I also pay health care contributions, a pension contribution, and union dues.

I was shocked at the difference when I received my first paycheck. This is important for anyone to understand when accepting a salary and budgeting for the month. That $1,473.58 difference changes where I can live, the daycare we can afford, and even eliminates my ability to indulge in Starbucks every day.

47

Saving for Retirement

Saving for retirement might seem odd to think about as a young adult. Can't that wait until you're thirty, forty, fifty, sixty? No! If you wait that long, you will miss out on years of opportunity to invest and save drastically more.

When you start a new job, many companies will offer a 401(k)-benefit program. This is the most common retirement plan. Your chosen contribution is automatically deducted from each paycheck and put into long-term investments that grow the account over time. The money in your 401(k) depends upon how much you contribute and how the investments perform.

One of the many benefits of a 401(k) program is the company match. About 50% of companies will offer to match a portion of your contribution. This is free money for you. The average match is 3% of your salary. Some companies will match 50% of your contribution up to a limit, and others will choose a percentage match based upon the company's annual performance.

The IRS sets a maximum yearly contribution limit, which is $20,500 for 2022 in addition to the employer match (if you are over 50, you can contribute a bit more). How the money is invested is mostly within your control. Your employer will offer a choice of several investment options managed by a financial services advisory group such as The Vanguard Group. You can choose one or several funds to invest in. Like any investment, there is some risk involved, but since this is a long-term investment, there is less risk if invested properly. I always suggest investing in the S&P 500 (America's five-hundred largest publicly traded companies).

401(k) plans also have special tax benefits. The contribution to your 401(k) is taken before tax, which lowers your taxable income and can put you in a lower tax bracket. When you withdraw the funds after retirement, you will pay the tax then, but most likely at a lower rate since you will no longer be working.

If you work for a non-profit or government organization, you will be offered a 403(b) or 457 plan instead of a 401(k), but the funds function the same way. Even better, 457 plans are penalty-free if you withdraw the money early. In addition, some companies now offer what is called a Designated Roth 401(k), which invests after-tax dollars.

Very few companies offer pensions anymore, but it is still popular among union jobs. A pension is a retirement fund in which you are automatically enrolled. Your employer makes contributions in addition to your mandated ones. Many people who have a pension still enroll in another retirement plan.

Finally, you can invest in a Roth IRA. Rather than payroll deductions, you make contributions to this type of fund on your own. A Roth IRA is invested just like a 401(k), but Roth IRA contributions are made with after-tax dollars. You pay the tax upfront, so your earnings are not taxed as they are for a 401(k). Many people use a Roth IRA in addition to another plan because the contribution limit in 2022 is $6,000 (or $7,000 if over fifty). The money you contribute to a Roth IRA decreases the amount you can contribute to your 401(k) since the $20,500 cap is for your retirement funds combined.

If you have a rainy-day fund and can cover your expenses, putting your other savings into a retirement account is a very prudent financial decision. I recommend that you contribute at least as much as the employer match for your 401(k). The chart below illustrates why saving for retirement now is financially savvy. It shows what your retirement investment will be worth after thirty-seven years of annual compounding with an initial deposit of zero dollars. I use an annual interest rate of

11.4%, which is the average rate of return when investing in the S&P 500 over the long term:

Annual Deposit	Employer Match (25%)	Total Savings after 37 years
$1,000 (About $19 a week)	$250	$650,981.87
$2,000 (About $38 a week)	$500	$1,301,963.75
$5,000 (About $96 a week)	$1,250	$3,254,909.37 (You read that right— **over $3 million!**)

The value of compounding is real! Want to retire a millionaire? You can do it! The takeaway? $1,000 sitting in a very low-earning savings account is better used in a retirement plan earning more money for later (just remember there is still some risk since you are investing in the stock market).

Want to retire a millionaire? You can do it!

What if you have an emergency and need your money earlier? Although you cannot withdraw from these accounts until you are fifty-nine-and-a-half, there is the option to withdraw early and pay a penalty. Most penalties include paying a tax as well as a 10% fee. You also have the option to borrow from yourself and pay it back over time, penalty-free.

In certain situations, you can withdraw early *without a penalty* or *need to pay yourself back*. These include qualifying college expenses, birth or adoption expenses, unreimbursed medical bills, health insurance premiums while unemployed, or disability-related expenses. Some hardships such as home repairs or funeral costs might also qualify. In the case of a Roth IRA, you can withdraw penalty-free for your first home purchase. Additionally, you will avoid the tax on your Roth IRA if your first contribution was made five or more years prior.

Simply put, you can access that money if you need it. Do not let fear keep you from starting to save for your retirement. Investing for retirement now is something you will thank your younger self for later.

COURTNEY COMMENT

If my dad weren't my dad, I wouldn't have even thought about opening a retirement fund at this point in my life. Let's get my kids through college first! But think about how much time, and money, I would have missed out on by waiting. I hope you can start your fund now, like me, and take this advice seriously.

Spend long workdays daydreaming about retiring on a beach with a fruity drink in hand? After seeing that calculation, I will be trying to contribute $5,000 a year to my fund so maybe that beach will be my own private island. God bless the power of compounding. Retirement, here I come!

48

The Stock Market

Investing money in the stock market can be a great opportunity. Unfortunately, many people treat the stock market like a game of Monopoly or a wild night on the Vegas strip. Investing is neither fake money nor reckless gambling. Investing, if done logically and purposefully, can grow your wealth exponentially.

It is important to be patient and detached.

Never put your hard-earned money into something you don't understand. If you are going to invest money in the stock market, whether through your retirement fund, a college fund, or savings, you should make sure you completely understand how the market works and where the money is invested. When you are new to investing in the stock market, ask for help, read about it, and seek guidance. Never invest money that you might need in the short-term (you pay lower taxes on your earnings if you wait at least twelve months to withdraw). Your rainy-day fund, for example, is not the money that you want to put into the stock market.

In this chapter, I overview the stock market and in the following chapter I get a bit more specific. The **stock market** refers to the buying and selling of **securities**, which are investments such as stocks and bonds that can be traded or exchanged for cash. The buying and selling takes place electronically at places called **exchanges**. There are different sellers, such as the NASDAQ and the New York Stock Exchange.

Stocks

A **stock** is an investment in a company. When you buy a stock, it's as though you own a piece of that company, which is called **equity**. Only publicly traded companies are part of the stock market, so you can't use this method to invest in the local Mom and Pop shop down the street. **As the company's fortune rises or falls, the stock price goes up or down, and your shares either gain or lose value in correlation.** When investing in stocks, your goal is to buy a stock at a low price and sell when the price is high to earn that difference. If you understand the market and you really believe in one particular company, you know the product well, and you think it'll grow, then you might consider investing in that one stock.

Bonds

A **bond** is another investment that represents a loan made by an investor to a borrower. When you buy a bond, you are in essence entering into a contract to loan money and receive that loan back plus interest on a specific future date. The borrower is typically a corporate or government group, which makes bonds relatively safe. The bond will clearly state the interest rate and the date at which you will get your return. The group issuing the bond sets the loan price and interest rate. If you hold onto a bond, you are guaranteed the money back if the borrower stays afloat. Bonds are rated by risk. I only invest in top-rated bonds, which are ones with the least risk of defaulting.

Lower Your Risk

Beyond investing in one stock or bond, you can do what is called **diversification** and invest in a group of securities. It is a wise decision to invest this way. This is called a **stock fund**. A stock fund is an investment in a group of stocks, which lowers your risk since the investment is in multiple companies and not dependent upon just one company's performance (you can also do this with bonds). Stock funds are often packaged together based on their capitalization (large-cap, mid-cap, and small-cap). Large-cap stocks typically grow slower but more consistently. My recommended investment fund is a large-cap referred to as the S&P 500, which is an investment in the five-hundred largest publicly traded US companies. History shows that this fund consistently performs well over time. From 1976-2020, it grew at an average 11.4% rate, meaning your investment doubles about every six to seven years.

Ride it Out

When you do invest, it is important to be patient and detached. Over one-hundred years, the stock market always averages up, but there will be many times in that period when it goes down and your investments follow. It is even more important to hold onto your investments then. Don't be impulsive and sell your stocks when the market is low to avoid losing more. They will trend up eventually. **You only lose if you take the money out.** You will have years where your investments struggle, but if you ride out these dips, the market will recover and eventually go even higher.

I lost a lot of money in the stock market on two different occasions because I did not follow this advice. When the stock market was tanking in 2002 and again in 2009, I watched my investment portfolios very closely. I saw my stock funds going down daily with the market's plummet. Foolishly, I took my money out when the stock market was down 40% because I didn't want to lose any more money, and as a result, I didn't get the benefit of the eventual rebound that always comes after a setback in the market. I learned my lesson, and now I invest unemotionally and do not check the funds daily. I look at the bigger picture.

What if you need the money at a certain point, but the market is in a recession? This is why understanding your investment is important. There are different ways to invest. For example, investing in a retirement or education/529 fund allows you to choose a portfolio that uses riskier investments in the beginning years but becomes more and more conservative as you get closer to the collection year. As that date approaches, less of your money should be in the market and more should be safe. This way, even if the market is in a recession when you retire, you still have plenty of earlier earnings.

Any investment will have some degree of risk. But the stock market doesn't have to be a gamble. The more you know about investing, the better you can grow your savings and choose the "safest" risk for the reward.

COURTNEY COMMENT

I am not going to lie (although I probably should)—I have an economics degree and I still don't understand the stock market. Investing feels intimidating, confusing, and, frankly, hard to trust. Do I really want to put my hard-earned money (of which I have little) into what feels like a high-stakes lottery ticket? Lottery tickets are fun, but only when the risk is low.

Therein lies my problem: I am thinking of the stock market like the lottery.

In the research and discussion for this section of the book, I realized that my equating the stock market to the lottery is an emotion-based attitude rather than an evidence-based one. Now I understand that when invested correctly, I'm not gambling my money. Rather, I'm taking on a small risk for a big return, especially if I'm investing my 401(k) in those large-cap funds (where I recognize most of the companies and use their products), and my investment plan gets less risky the closer I get to retirement.

This is smart, not crazy.

Still, I struggle with completely trusting the market and taking on even a small financial risk. I still sometimes picture the market as that unreliable on-again-off-again boyfriend who looks pretty but continually lets you down. Hopefully, time and experience will build my confidence, or else I'm kicking it to the curb like I did that ex!

I encourage you to start investing small with me so we can overcome the fear and enjoy the reward together (and by reward, I mean fancy cocktails paid for by our stock dividends!). I'll meet you at the bar!

49

Mastering the Stock Market: Penny Stocks and Limit Orders

Controlling your emotions and impulses is key to conquering the stock market. As you begin to invest, you will surely come across penny stocks, and they will be tempting! Penny stocks are small company stocks priced at less than five dollars a share. They aren't liquid since they're rarely sold by a major stock exchange (and therefore most likely won't have buyers readily available when you need to sell). Their allure? They're cheap. The gains can be large, but the risks of losing a significant amount of money in a short period is even larger.

My advice? Stay away from them...always! Buy stock in real companies instead. There are reasons why a stock is a penny stock. Fraud is a possibility. Bankruptcy is very probable. And it is very difficult to make an informed decision when buying a penny stock because it is often impossible to track down the company's financial data.

I hear the same story time and time again—someone learns something about a stock and swears that it's going to skyrocket and get them rich quick. I myself have lived it. What have I learned? By the time the average person hears about a stock like this, they are too late to reap the benefits.

This was the case when I ignored all reason and invested in a penny stock about fifteen years ago. I was sucked into a story, believing I had enough information and guidance to make a wise investment. I learned the hard way that such a thing does not exist when dealing with a penny stock.

How did it happen? The mother of one of my employees came into the office during lunch one day with a check in the amount of his entire bank account earned from years of birthday and graduation money. He was using this money, in addition to maxing out three credit cards, to invest in a penny stock called Sovereign Exploration Associates International, Inc. This company was in the business of locating and recovering historically significant sunken ships. My employee shared that Sovereign had obtained the license for an area off the coast of Halifax where a British warship called the HMS *Fantome* was identified. This fleet sunk in the treacherous waters south of Halifax during the War of 1812 after looting the White House, the US Treasury, and the Capitol. Sovereign was prepared to recover artifacts that could include gold and paper seals. They were waiting for the waters to warm to bring up the *Fantome*. Then the stock price would soar.

**Controlling your emotions and impulses is key
to conquering the stock market.**

I was a history major in college and captivated by the story. The stock was only twenty-three cents a share, and I kept researching and following it as the tales of the *Fantome* played out in my head night after night. The icing on the cake? By a strange coincidence, I learned that my accountant happened to be the CFO of the company. When I called him, I learned that he believed the investment in this penny stock would be a home run, and he opted to take all his fees in equity. My accountant is conservative, so I took the plunge and invested.

Where is that money now? At the bottom of the ocean with the *Fantome*. It is worth zero dollars! Before the ship could be brought up, the British government claimed ownership since it was their ship. Nova Scotian officials accepted this without due process, so Sovereign sued the Province of Nova Scotia. The US government also claimed ownership since everything on board was their property. The company ultimately chose to not recover the ship and went out of business.

If you learn anything from this crazy story, I hope it is to stay away from penny stocks. Nothing is a sure deal! Make smart, clear-headed, and safe investments.

To help you manage your investments safely, you can use limit orders. This is my final tip when it comes to investing. If you believe a particular stock is a good investment (*not* a penny stock), you can put into place a buy limit order through your financial institution. This is a directive to purchase the stock if it hits a specific price. You don't want to buy the stock for the list price. Wait, watch, and buy low.

For example, I really like a company called 3M. They have a lot of cash and pay shareholders a dividend every three months that has increased for thirty straight years. 3M was trading at $219 a share in 2018. I liked the stock but didn't want to buy at that price. I put in a buy limit order for $186.15 (15% lower than listed), held for sixty days. If the stock fell there or below, I would automatically purchase shares. I ended up investing at $183 a share. The price is now up to $199, and with the dividends I collect and re-invest, those shares are worth more now than when I bought them.

There are also sell limit orders. This is an order to sell a stock if it goes up to a certain price. For example, if 3M goes up over 20% of what I paid for it, then I have a sell limit order for it to be sold. I bought and sold JetBlue stock four different times this way as it kept increasing to my sell limit order.

Using limit orders takes the emotion out of overseeing your investments and allows you to set rules to help manage your stocks rationally. With these few tips, you can successfully handle your investments.

COURTNEY COMMENT

Come on, Dad, really?! A sunken pirate ship?

My dad didn't want me to make the same investment mistakes he did. He let me pick out a stock at a young age to learn about investing wisely. I loved Limited Too (a kids clothing store) and chose its stock, not realizing they also owned Victoria's Secret and other adult clothing stores. I did well without realizing the stock's potential. Obviously, it wasn't a penny stock.

We paid $2,000 for the stock, I received small dividends over the years, and then I received over $10,000 when I later sold the stock. I used that money to decorate my first apartment. Clearly, I learned at a young age that good investments pay off. I'll sit out on the penny stocks for now and watch my dad as he waits for the ship to be brought to the surface.

50

What Are You Worth?

At any given time, it is important to know your net worth. This means knowing exactly how much money you have left once you pay off all your debt.

It can be a frightening figure, especially if you have large student loans, a car payment, and credit card debt. Your debt might be larger than your assets or capital, meaning you owe more money than you have. That's okay! Knowing exactly what you owe in relation to how much money you have is a powerful tool to help set goals and make smart spending decisions to get back in the green!

Knowing exactly what you owe in relation to how much money you have is a powerful tool to help set goals and make smart spending decisions.

As a young adult, I started tracking my net worth monthly, and I still do this today. I suggest picking a consistent day of the month to do this calculation. I use the first of the month since my investment funds and bonds pay their dividends then.

When I began tracking my net worth, Michele and I had little in the way of assets. We had a car, some sports memorabilia, some wedding money, and a small savings fund. We also had debt. Fast forward to today, and this knowledge helped me pay off all my debt, send my children to college, and save for my retirement.

The process is a monthly reality check! Seeing my net worth regularly, especially as a young adult, inspired me to pay down my debt early and make informed monthly spending decisions. If I wanted to buy a new suit, for example, I held off until we were out of the red (our worth was a positive number).

Your net worth is a simple calculation:

Net Worth = Your Assets − Your Debt

I keep track of this data using pen and paper, but there are apps that can do it for you.

What are some of the big items to include in your net worth calculation?

Common Assets

- Savings (cash totals in bank accounts)
- Retirement funds
- Investments (e.g., IRA, life insurance policy, bonds)
- Personal property (e.g., collectibles, jewelry, boat)
- Businesses
- Home/land (-6% selling fee)

Common Debt

- Credit Cards
- Car loans
- College loans

If you have a mortgage on a property, I advise you to list your investment as an asset since you can sell the property to eliminate the debt. Therefore, the value of your property is an asset (total asset = down payment + money paid toward principal + increase in home value). The one caveat? List this sum with 6% subtracted to cover the real estate fees you would incur if selling the property.

You can include your vehicle in your net worth if you buy your car rather than lease it. You determine how much equity you have in your car by looking up the value of your car in the Kelley Blue Book and subtracting how much you owe on it. The difference can be included under your assets or as debt, depending upon that total.

Once your net worth calculation is complete, take the opportunity to evaluate which assets and debt increased or decreased, if your investments performed well, and the goals you have for the upcoming month. Look at your worth alongside your monthly budget to see the bigger picture along with the smaller one.

Many people feel overwhelmed facing the reality of their financial situation. However, you cannot thoughtfully plan for your future until you do so. Take the plunge, set your goals, and make those dreams of financial independence come true one month at a time.

COURTNEY COMMENT

Want to digitally track your net worth?

Personal Capital is a popular app that can do it for you. You connect the account to your credit cards, bank accounts, loan accounts, retirement funds, and investments to update your net worth in real time. They create charts and graphs with an analysis of your spending and investing. All of this is available in their free version, and users rave about their easy-to-use dashboard and safety. My brother uses it and loves it (and no, I swear this is not a paid advertisement).

Whether you write it out or leave it to the robo-Gods to compute, the takeaway's the same: know your financial livelihood and use that information to inform your decisions.

51

Cars: Lease or Buy?

An automobile is often your first big purchase. Unless you live in a major city with public transportation, you will probably need a car.

In purchasing a car, I advise you to consider safety as a foremost concern. Check the safety rating and be cautious with the history of a used car. Auto accidents are too common, and if you ever suffer such a catastrophe, you want to make sure your vehicle can protect you. No matter how inexpensive a car might be, your life is not worth gambling.

> **When you are ready to make a decision,**
> **remember that everything is negotiable.**

When you are ready to buy a car, understand the costs that come in addition to a monthly payment so that you are financially prepared. You will need to pay for car insurance, maintenance, and gas (check the car's average miles/gallon). Budget for these expenses. Then, do your research to figure out the right car for both you and your wallet.

Narrow down a list of potential cars and then test drive your top contenders. Keep in mind that once you complete a test drive, salespeople will pressure you to buy a car. To keep the dealers in check, tell them upfront that you are looking at many different cars and will not be ready to make a decision for a few months. **Don't buy a car on the spot if you want to get the best price.**

Once you have determined which car is right for you, decide if you will lease it, buy new, or buy used. There are pros and cons to each scenario.

Leasing

Leasing a car is like renting a house: you make monthly payments to use it, but you do not build equity. A lease is a contract that allows you to use a car for a certain period, usually two to four years. The vehicle remains under warranty during the lease period, so you don't need to worry about anything except routine maintenance.

Leasing is a great option for someone who likes to get a new car every few years. Leases usually have lower monthly payments than a car loan, so you can afford a nicer car. But, beware, leasing costs more in the long run and often comes with more fees and penalties. You also have a yearly mileage limit and are charged a per mile fee if you go over this limit. Additionally, it is difficult to get out of a lease if your income suddenly changes and you can no longer afford the vehicle.

Buying New

Buying a new car, on the other hand, allows you to make monthly payments that eventually end with you owning the car. Therefore, you can customize it and drive as many miles as you want! If you plan to keep your car for a long time, buying is a great option because once you pay off the loan, the car is yours with no further payments.

You can then trade the car in for money. Understanding your car's resale value is important. If you choose to purchase a car, your monthly payments will be higher because they are based on the total value of the car whereas lease payments are based off the devaluation. Finally, when you buy, you must be prepared to cover repair costs once the warranty expires.

Buying Used

If you plan to buy a used car, you can get great deals, but be careful. Use online sites such as cars.com, Edmonds, consumer reports, and Kelley

Blue Book to research the vehicle. Get the VIN number of the car to see if it was in any previous accidents. Assess how many miles it has, previous owners, and why it is being sold. Ask when it was last in for maintenance and if anything needs to be repaired. Again, your safety and your investment are both important to protect.

When you are ready to make your decision, remember that everything is negotiable: the features, the overall price, the monthly payment—you name it! I recommend bringing someone with you who understands cars. Also, shop around to get the best price.

My son decided on a Nissan Altima for his first car. It had a five-star safety rating, four doors, and four cylinders, so we were supportive of the decision (a safe, slow car!). When it came time to make the purchase, we sat down and identified every Nissan dealer within a fifty-mile radius and called each one. We asked directly for the general manager—that is the person who can make deals. We were upfront with what we were looking for and told every dealer we wanted their best and final price. Most dealers were within a couple hundred dollars of each other, but one was $1,200 less. That dealership was the highest-selling Nissan dealership in the state the previous month, so corporate awarded them added incentives to use on competitive deals. When you make these calls, you might be able to get a better deal if you are flexible on features. Courtney's husband paid a few thousand dollars less on his first car by purchasing it in brown.

Whether you choose to lease or buy, you will set up financing to determine your monthly payments. This is the last step in the process. When you set up your financing, you determine how many months your payments will span. I recommend never going longer than sixty months. You will also be offered after-purchase add-ons such as fabric and paint protection, extended warranties, and tire and wheel packages. These are often marked up and have a lot of fine print. You might also be asked to buy upgrades such as all-weather mats and tinted windows. Always try to get these items thrown in for free or shop the price elsewhere.

Buying a car is an exciting endeavor. Do your research and then you can make the best choice for yourself as well as enjoy the process.

COURTNEY COMMENT

When picking out a car, here are some "fun" facts to keep in mind:[3]

- Black cars are the least likely to get pulled over (even though it is the most common car color)
- Red cars are a ticket magnet
- Luxury coupes and sporty sedans receive the most tickets, while family friendly sedans, SUVs, and minivans receive the least
- Pickups, Camrys, and Civics are among the top cars stolen
- Toyotas and Hondas tend to last the longest and are some of the safest cars
- L Certified by Lexus is one of the Best CPO programs

---

[3] Scott Huntington, "It's Not a Myth: Certain Colors and Makes Get Pulled Over More Often," National Motorists Association Blog, February 9, 2016, https://www.motorists.org/blog/get-pulled-over-more-often/. Last accessed July 30, 2021.

52

Home: Rent or Buy?

The dream of home ownership is deeply ingrained in American society. From the pursuit of manifest destiny to the multimillion-dollar HGTV network, Americans have obsessed over owning property for centuries. But is this a realistic dream? Is it even a beneficial one? Or is it simply a misguided obsession?

If you have accomplished the goal of being able to support yourself and live independently, the choice to rent or buy is an important consideration. Your first step is to determine if you have a choice at all. To own a home, you must be able to obtain a mortgage loan. Do you qualify for one? How much do you qualify for? If you do not qualify for a mortgage, then you cannot buy a property unless you use a co-signer who agrees to make the payments if you are unable. It might be better to rent and save for your future home in that scenario. If you do qualify for a mortgage, make sure you have enough savings for the purchase. When purchasing a home, putting down 20% of the purchase price is standard to avoid additional fees. Buying property with less down or even no down payment could be an option, but you will have a higher interest rate and fees, which might not be a good decision in the long run.

I believe home ownership is still an admirable goal if it is a properly informed decision. Yet, renting has benefits too. There are many reasons to rent instead of buy.

Benefits of Renting

- Easier to relocate
- Lower upfront costs
- Lower monthly bills
- Less responsibility (landlord is responsible for maintenance)

On the flip side, the disadvantages of renting are twofold. First, you have no control. You cannot change anything in the home without permission. If your lease is not renewed, you will be forced to move. Additionally, you do not have the opportunity to build equity when you pay rent. Money paid to your landlord is money you will never see again.

Buying a property, in my opinion, is a better financial decision if you can afford it and the timing is right.

Benefits of Buying

- Investment opportunity
- Stability
- Control
- Tax incentives
- Building equity
- Predictable payments

If you have the money for a down payment and money saved for maintenance emergencies (you don't want to be house poor), buying a home is a great investment opportunity. But you must be certain that the home you want to buy is an investment and not a liability. To make a good investment, you need a good deal. Work with a realtor that you trust who will allow you to negotiate. It is also important to understand the marketplace. To gain value on your home, you want to make the purchase during a buyer's market. Location is important as well. Buy in an area that will add to the home's value.

My nephew and his wife made a great investment on their first home. They bought a new construction apartment in the up-and-coming neighborhood of Southie in Boston. Two years later, it sold in just twenty-four hours for $85,000 more than the purchase price; with their down payment and equity, they walked away with $150,000 and were able to pay off their student loans!

Owning a home offers you and your family stability. You have a community in which to plant roots and the freedom to make any changes you want.

Home ownership also awards you tax advantages. Although there aren't as many as in the past, one advantage remains: there is no capital gains tax paid on your profit when you sell your house, up to $250,000 for a single person and $500,000 for a married couple.

**Home ownership is still an admirable goal
if it is a properly informed decision.**

The last benefit is equity. A major difference between renting and buying is where your monthly payments go. When you buy, you essentially pay yourself each month. Paying your mortgage is akin to forced savings. When you sell your house, you will hopefully get that money back and more if the investment was a good one. Also, your rent could increase each year, but your mortgage stays consistent and predictable.

The downside of home ownership is that you are responsible for the maintenance. If you need a new roof, for example, you might end up needing to spend thousands of dollars to cover the cost. There are also many upfront costs.

Deciding whether to rent or buy depends upon your timing and personal situation. Only you can decide what's right. Assess your priorities, follow the market, and review your opportunities to make the best choice.

COURTNEY COMMENT

Home ownership is difficult, even impossible, for many people. It is much easier if you come from a privileged background, and I don't ever want to take for granted that I had help to purchase my first home. Most people need to rent for decades to save up for a home. That is the norm. I do not think owning a home has to be an end goal; having a safe place to live, wherever it is, is a major accomplishment.

PART FIVE

HEALTH AND RELATIONSHIPS

Here you are, at section five, the final section of the book. If you read the book in order, congratulations on making it this far. If you are starting here, welcome!

You will notice a shift in tone and style as we move from straightforward advice to nuanced personal guidance. Just as your personal life might sometimes be messy and emotional, so is this section. It will sometimes feel confessional and diaristic, but it will still have clear tips for success.

Why the change? Your personal life is the most important to develop, and we hope that opening up to you will help you to examine your own life so that you can grow. When you develop the personal, you will thrive professionally and be your best overall self.

53

Know Your Family History

Our families influence us through nature as well as nurture. You might
be kind like your mother or love chess like your father. Perhaps you
inherited your blue eyes and height from your grandparents. Some influences can be controlled, while others cannot.

When discussing genetics, people often fixate on who they resemble.
What they fail to recognize is the diseases they could have inherited as
well. Who wants to discuss Grandma's cancer or Dad's bipolar disorder?
It's uncomfortable enough to talk about another person's health issues
but even more challenging when considering that you might be at higher
risk for them. It's essential to push through the discomfort, as this information is critical to understand and use wisely.

In the beginning of the 1900s, the average American lived into their
early forties. When Franklin Roosevelt established social security about
forty years later, the average life expectancy was sixty-two. Today, the
average life span is eighty-one, almost doubling in just over one-hundred
years. Medical advancements have resulted in a greater prolongment of
life, and it will only keep getting longer. If you want to benefit from this,
it is imperative that you understand the diseases for which you're at a
higher risk.

There are many ways to reduce your risk of disease regardless of genetics: being mindful of diet, exercising regularly, and not smoking, to name a few. But awareness of your family history and taking appropriate preventative measures are the best ways to mitigate diseases such as cancer, diabetes, blood pressure, mental health, heart disease, and stroke.

It's important to collect your family's medical history as soon as possible. Talk to your birth parents and older relatives on both sides of your family. If someone in your family died at an early age, understand their cause of death. Take notice of diseases that affected multiple family members and discover the age in which the disease developed. A complete record would cover three generations and include grandparents, parents, children, brothers and sisters, aunts and uncles, nieces and nephews, and cousins.

The earlier you know your genetic predispositions, the more opportunity you have to decrease your risk.

Once you have this information and understand your risk, it's crucial to share it with your physician. A medical expert can provide resources and create a plan for monitoring and prevention. The earlier you know your genetic predispositions, the more opportunity you have to decrease your risk. For example, you can get regular screenings at an earlier age if a certain cancer runs in your family. You can't change your genes, but you can change your behavior.

Awareness of my family medical history saved my life. My dad died in his fifties from a heart attack, and I have multiple uncles who had fatal heart attacks, too. When I turned fifty, my wife insisted I undergo a cardiac CAT scan because of this history. I was instantly sent for a stress test following the scan. I thought I aced it—I wasn't even sweating! I couldn't have been more wrong.

They identified two blockages in the arteries of my heart. One of those arteries is referred to as the widow maker because so many people die from heart attacks caused by this type of blockage. I had a 75% blockage in both arteries and no symptoms. I could have died at any moment. I was directed to get surgery immediately. I wanted second opinions, but there was no time. Stents were inserted into the blocked arteries, and I was out the next day. The day after I went home, I was walking and coaching a little league baseball game. Again, modern medicine is remarkable and can greatly prolong your life if you take precautionary actions. If I didn't know my family history, I don't think I would have scheduled that scan, and I might not be here today.

It might not be as much fun to brag about your risk of developing high blood pressure as it is your long line of musical talent, but it could greatly lengthen your life. The sooner you have these discussions, the sooner you can start taking preventative measures.

COURTNEY COMMENT

"I got it from my mama" takes on a whole different meaning when it comes to family medical history.

For females, there are genetic diseases that preventative measures can greatly impact. Breast cancer, ovarian cancer, and depression are some examples.

For males, heart disease, prostate cancer, and depression have strong genetic components.

Mental health is often overlooked when discussing family history, but it can be hereditary. In my family, there is a lot of mental illness: alcoholism, drug addiction, depression, anxiety, and bipolar disorder. Luckily, when I had my first panic attack, I was aware of the symptoms and had my family to help in the journey.

Knowledge is power. Still, the fear of the "what ifs" can be paralyzing. What if I also die young of a heart attack? What if I develop Alzheimer's? Seeing our loved ones suffer from a disease and knowing it might also be our fate is frightening. But armed with the knowledge, you can prevent and mitigate your risk. So go, get it from your mama, and plan from there!

54

Be an Active Participant in Your Healthcare

Ultimately, your health is your responsibility. Doctors are professionals and share advice, but the choices you make with the information are yours. You must take control of your healthcare.

Schedule a yearly physical to stay on top of your health. Most insurance plans cover an annual check-up. Many people (myself included, until I met Michele) only go to a doctor if something is wrong. This is a mistake. Just like a car needs yearly maintenance, you too need regular well-visits. There are often issues under the hood that only a professional can identify.

Empower yourself and be the one in charge of your body.

Build a relationship with your doctor; make sure they have a health baseline and full family history. When you do get sick, your doctor will then be able to compare your symptoms with your norm, and you'll already have a relationship established. My rapport with my primary care physician is critical to my health maintenance. He monitors my PSA numbers for prostate cancer, my heart health, and everything in between.

It is important to be open with your doctor and share any concerns. Do not be embarrassed—doctors have seen it all! They have the knowledge to detect illness earlier than you can, and early detection makes a major difference in your prognosis. I encourage you to bring questions to your doctor. I have my physical coming up and already have a list of questions about the vitamins I take, a pill for uric acid, my low heart rate, vaccines, my LDL, and sun exposure.

It is also important to understand the measurements your doctor uses to monitor your heart health. They take your blood pressure, which is given in two numbers. Your goal is for your blood pressure to be less than 120/80. Cholesterol is another common indicator of heart health. You have good (HDL) and bad (LDL) cholesterol. Your goal is to have an HDL of forty or higher for men and fifty or higher for women, and an LDL of less than one hundred.

Staying on top of your healthcare and understanding your role versus the doctor's will help you better navigate serious medical problems.

As a child, I struggled with knee issues. I was a competitive basketball player and very active. In high school, I suffered a severe knee injury, and my mother took me for an evaluation with a surgeon. The doctor said he could repair my knee and I'd be back on the court in six weeks, but the injury could reoccur. He informed us of a new surgery where he would remove my entire kneecap and I would never suffer the same injury again. He gave me a 99.9% assurance that I could return to athletics and went on to claim that this is the surgery he would perform if he had a son in my position. My parents believed you always do what the doctors advise, so we proceeded with this "innovative" surgery.

Sadly, it was a failure. I was in a leg cast for three and a half months and went through a long rehab. I could never run the same again, and my athletic career was over. They removed my kneecap and did not replace it with an artificial joint. I can walk and exercise, but my leg does not bend naturally. I found out many years later that this surgery was performed for a few months and never used again.

The price I paid for this mistake was large, but I learned a lot from the experience. Don't ever let someone cut into you without knowing all the facts! Find the right doctor—bedside manner does not make someone the best at what they do. I never again let a doctor determine my next steps without asking many, many questions. I always get two or three professional opinions and do my own homework and research. I am now the one who ultimately makes decisions about my body.

In 2014, I was diagnosed with prostate cancer, and I took complete control of my treatment. Because of my family history, I'd been screening for prostate cancer for years and caught it early. I researched and found the best surgeon in the Philadelphia area and read everything that I could about my options.

My PSA numbers were not exceptionally high; however, I later learned that was not necessarily indicative of a less aggressive cancer. The surgeon suggested scheduling surgery immediately. I wanted to delay it a few months to get in the best shape I could. He saw no harm in a delay, so we rescheduled. Having this extra time allowed me to prepare physically and mentally. I was also really concerned about having a catheter in my penis after surgery and read that doctors could instead use what is called a suprapubic catheter and go through my belly button. My surgeon did not commonly do this, so I had to advocate for myself to have it. In the end, he used the suprapubic catheter, and it majorly impacted my mental and physical recovery. I am now cancer-free and proud of the role I played in my journey.

At the end of the day, you are the person most invested in your health. You know yourself best. Empower yourself and be the one in charge of your body.

COURTNEY COMMENT

If you ever have the opportunity to meet my dad in person, ask to see his left knee—it is completely flat with a gnarly scar. You could actually rest a cup on it. You cannot make this stuff up.

What else can't you make up? Implicit bias. We judge others all the time without realizing it. Statistically, doctors make assumptions about patients' health based on biases such as weight, race, gender, and age. Women and nonwhite patients are often misdiagnosed.[1]

I have personally faced weight bias, but I have learned many ways to advocate for myself in the healthcare space. What do I do?

- Call ahead to see if the doctor has plus-size gowns, and if not, I bring my own
- If my doctor suggests weight loss as a remedy for an issue I am having, I ask what they would suggest for a lower-weight patient with the same ailment
- I bypass the scale (that is your right)

I am always clear with my doctors that I don't want weight to be the topic of conversation since I am recovering from an eating disorder. You can be upfront with your doctor about all of your treatment concerns. The right doctor for you will listen. My mom has hypochondriasis, fear of illness, and she always tells her providers upfront that they need to be careful about how they discuss her treatment.

There are many ways you can advocate for yourself to make your patient experience better and receive the treatment you deserve.

---

[1] American College of Cardiology, "Implicit Bias: Recognizing the Unconscious Barriers to Quality Care and Diversity in Medicine," *Cardiology Magazine* 49, no. 1 (2020): 22–25.

55

Ditch Dieting

Physically, I reached my healthiest self in the last ten years. I spent so much time during my younger life on and off diets. I tried everything from Weight Watchers to Nutrisystem, hoping to find an answer to how to lose weight. If I could go back and change things, I would. Diets don't work, although that's not what popular culture tells us.

Weight loss products make up one of the biggest markets out there. Everyone wants the quick fix and will shell out lots of money to get it. Ironically, what keeps this industry in business is the fact that you will be a returning customer. If you are like me, weight loss programs help you slim down in the short term, but you always end up gaining the weight back, and then some. This is called yo-yo dieting, and it's an easy cycle in which to be trapped. Depriving yourself simply doesn't work!

Obsessing over what you eat can be dangerous to your health and lead you back to the diet trap time and time again. But how you eat helps with behavioral changes.

What I have learned, and what I attribute my ability to maintain a healthy weight to (finally!), is that nutrition is all about fueling my body and feeling satisfied, feeling nourished. For me, I like simplicity. This means relying on specific foods to feel satiated and energized: oatmeal, whole grains, fruit, yogurt.

I also focus on *how* I eat. Obsessing over *what* you eat can be dangerous to your health and lead you back to the diet trap time and time again. But *how* you eat helps with the behavioral changes necessary to maintain your health in the long run. I eat mindfully. As one of six kids, we grew up eating very fast. The more quickly you finished your plate, the more likely you were to get seconds. It took me a long time to change that habit. Now, I eat slowly and appreciate the food on my plate, giving my body time to process and enjoy it. The need to do everything quickly and efficiently is standing in your way of eating better. Changing how you eat is not easy, but it will do a lot more for your health than a diet.

I do not have a secret handbook for how to lose weight, and I can't promise you a smaller pant size like the diet commercials do, but I can promise you that there is a better way than dieting. And perhaps a smaller pant size isn't a healthy goal for everyone anyway. Clearly, there's a health crisis in America. The beauty standards in our culture have created immense pressure to look a certain way. Eating disorders are rampant, and psychological components, social media, and other societal pressures all contribute to the problem. There is no easy fix, and it is extremely complicated. I pass the torch to Courtney on this one to add more depth to the conversation.

COURTNEY COMMENT

The health chapters of this book have been the most difficult for me to write.

To be honest, I feel like a fraud. I am overweight and under-exercised. I have gained one-hundred pounds in eight years. And sadly, I feel like I must "confess" this to you. I lack energy and motivation. I went from a very fit, athletic, salad-eating vegetarian to an out-of-shape, overly stressed binge-eater in my post-college life. And sadly, once again, I feel like I need to talk about the beautiful, younger me to give me credibility. Will you like me better if you know I used to be "acceptable"?

These thoughts are indicative of how disordered my thinking is surrounding food and body. Why do I feel the need to apologize for taking up space? Why do so many of us feel this way?

In truth, I am on a journey. Like so many Americans, I have a lot to work out. It's complicated, like being in an open relationship with your ex-level complicated.

I have an eating disorder. It's been hard for me to admit this because being overweight is often considered a choice. How can "choosing to overindulge" be considered a disease? I am still working on accepting that.

Society celebrated me as a fit overachiever, but I was not healthy then either: I had so many rules surrounding what I could and couldn't eat. I feared certain foods. Lived with food guilt. Worked out twice a day. I restricted my eating. I was on and off diets. I never thought I was skinny enough. I never felt good enough. Who can maintain that way of living? Who would want to?

And now the pendulum has swung the other way. It is two sides of the same sick coin.

I am trying to find my balance, my happy medium. I am working with a dietician and therapist to understand my binge-eating disorder and heal my relationship with food. I am learning about intuitive eating and trying to embrace a *health at every size* mentality. It's empowering. And a relief!

I see my dad's eating as rigid, but I know it works for him, and I envy anyone who finds a way to be at peace with food. I am not there... yet. I am a work in progress. Many of my dad's thoughts, and even my own, are indicative of a greater cultural issue: fatphobia. Weight is not a proven indicator of health. We must shift our focus from shame to support. I am working to truly reject diet culture, and it is a lot more complicated than I can do justice in this small section.

Clearly, the work I need to do is within. Our shells are simply manifestations of a deeper suffering. I do not know where this journey ends or how I will look at the end of it, but I know that I will feel whole and beautiful and shame-free in whatever body stands at that finish line.

If you have these thoughts and have suffered from the expectations of society, family, friends, and self as I have, you are not alone. And I know how difficult it is. But your body is valid and allowed to exist just as you are right in this very moment—don't ever let anyone make you feel otherwise. Your worth has nothing to do with your weight.

I have nothing witty to add to this chapter. All I have is this, my vulnerable admittance to struggling myself. I hope that you will handle me gently as I heal. We all have our challenges, and in that we are human, in all our beautiful shapes and sizes. I love you in all your humanness, truly, and I am working toward loving me, too.

Need help with an eating disorder?
Visit www.nationaleatingdisorders.org/help-support/contact-helpline
to speak with a professional.

Want to learn more about intuitive eating and health at every size?
Read *Anti-Diet* by Christy Harrison.

56

Discover the Right Exercise for You

Movement is essential to your overall health, both physical and mental. When you are physically active, your body loosens, blood circulates, you build strength and endurance, endorphins are released that help boost mood and reduce stress, and you just feel better. If you struggle to incorporate regular activity into your life, you are not alone; however, if your goal is to strengthen your mental and physical health, exercise will help.

Like many people, I was an active child involved in many sports. Physical activity was enjoyable, natural, and fun. But when I started working, physical activity was put on the back burner. That is, until I found community and a program that worked for me.

The first time I was able to get regular physical activity back into my life was when I found a group of people from work to join me at the gym. It was the sense of community and accountability that made exercise easy and fun again. I highly recommend finding at least one other person to be your workout partner. These men are still some of my best friends.

"Walking is the best medicine."

—HIPPOCRATES

The other piece to the puzzle came way later in life. I had to find a fitness program that worked for me personally. You need to find an activity that you enjoy, or you'll lose interest. For me, I discovered circuit training.

I struggled with working out on my own because I get bored easily, especially if I'm doing forty-five minutes on a cardio machine. I spent a few days at a wellness retreat called Canyon Ranch about eight years ago where I was exposed to circuit training, and I was hooked! This is a workout where you go back and forth between aerobic exercise and strength training, switching every two minutes. I adapted this workout at home and never get bored because of how fast it moves. I can easily challenge myself or reduce the level depending on how I feel. I do a circuit every other day and let my muscles rest with light cardio or yoga on the other days.

The circuit was the answer for me. For you, it might be tennis, basketball, jogging, swimming, rowing, even ping pong. It is also helpful to incorporate walking into your daily routine. As Hippocrates said, "Walking is the best medicine."

The Department of Health and Human Services recommends healthy adults do a weekly total of 150 minutes of moderate aerobic activity, or 75 minutes of vigorous aerobic activity, in addition to two days of strength training.[2] If you can accomplish this goal, you will feel better, live longer, and have more energy.

---

[2] "American Heart Association Recommendations for Physical Activity in Adults and Kids," The American Heart Association, https://www.heart.org/en/healthy-living/fitness/fitness-basics/aha-recs-for-physical-activity-in-adults.

COURTNEY COMMENT

My exercise journey is also a complicated one.

During my childhood, my parents "suggested" we exercise a certain number of times per week. They had only pure intentions, hoping to instill the importance of fitness from a young age.

Unfortunately, this backfired. My siblings and I have the same story (although we didn't find out until years later that we had the same "trick"). We would go into the at-home exercise room, turn on the treadmill and the television, and put our feet on the outer rails, letting the machine run while we relaxed and enjoyed some Nickelodeon. At ten years old, I did not want to be on a treadmill.

Exercise became a chore rather than an enjoyable activity. My brother and I were athletes, and this extreme workout mentality stuck with us. There were times when I worked out three times a day (and was praised for it). I never missed a workout, especially when I was on vacation. I vigorously sat at the cardio equipment until I burned more calories than I ate. It didn't ever feel like a choice. Actually, I didn't know there was another way at the time.

Now, as a working adult, I am turned off by exercise because of the pressure I still feel. I am working on finding activity that is simply enjoyable and does not trigger the trauma of my past. I enjoy walking, yoga, and simple strength training equipment, but I find myself getting frustrated at my body for not being able to do what it used to and mad at myself if I don't stick to a consistent plan. And so, the trauma resurfaces. It's my baggage to unpack so I can enjoy the activity that my body craves.

I think it's really important to flip the script for our families. Encourage joyful movement and naturally incorporate that into your lives—a weekend hike, a walk around the neighborhood looking for wildlife, having a catch. I hope this is the mentality I can teach my kids and let them figure out training for a sport if they wish. I hope to break the cycle, and I know that if my dad could go back and do things differently, he would.

My advice? Find ways to personally enjoy movement. And for our younger kids—let them just play! I strongly encourage you to play, too.

Worried you might have an unhealthy relationship with exercise? Visit www.nationaleatingdisorders.org/learn/general-information/ compulsive-exercise to learn more.

57

Say Yes to Yoga

Yoga has ancient roots, with the first written record of the practice coming from India about two thousand years ago. Yoga is centered upon improving spiritual and mental energy through breathing. There are many types of yoga, and you can explore which classes and practices speak to you. Any yoga practice will incorporate a combination of holding specific poses and deep breathing.

It keeps me grounded, clear-headed, and energized.

I wish I had started practicing yoga earlier. It has improved my flexibility, back problems, and strength. More importantly, it keeps me grounded, clear-headed, and energized. There are numerous proven benefits: improved heart health, enhanced mood, reduced inflammation, improved lung function, better sleep, eased anxiety and depression, increased self-esteem, reduced migraines, and more.

I began taking yoga classes with my wife about twenty years ago. Our teacher, Mary Bode, helped me embark on this journey. She is currently in her nineties, still teaching, and healthy in both body and mind. And she is hilarious. There is no better testament for the power of yoga than that!

I stopped attending classes for several years and cultivated an at-home practice, but when I did return to class, it was of course to Mary. Me being who I am, I asked Mary if I could make an announcement before we started. I explained to a room full of women that Mary first introduced me to yoga. I told them that I've been traveling the world studying with greats like Swami Gandhi (a name I fabricated). I warned them they would see flexibility in my body that might overwhelm them, and it was quite possible that I would levitate. And it was all because of Mary, the greatest yoga instructor in the world! They looked stunned. As I struggled to touch my toes, everyone quickly realized I was not a trained yogi, and we broke out in laughter. And that's the heart of yoga—community, acceptance, connection, and love.

Many yoga classes end with the instructor putting their hands together, bowing, and saying, "Namaste." You might want to bow and say it back. A common interpretation of Namaste in the yoga community is "the divine light in me bows to the divine light within you." This phrase is a wonderful representation of what's at the heart of the practice, finding that spark within yourself and acknowledging that greatness in others. It's what makes us beautiful and connects us all.

Although yoga can be spiritual, it can also be very physical. Many classes will leave you sweating and feeling strong. Yoga is a wonderful way to honor your body and all it can do.

Since I began practicing, I've been able to share this gift with many people and watch it help them. My company has a yoga studio next door, and two days a week we have an instructor offer free yoga classes to our employees. It increases our productivity to take the time away from our desks to practice. Two of our employees went on to become yoga teachers.

If you want to give yoga a try but don't know where or how to start, I recommend asking for a free trial class at a local studio or using the free and highly rated app **Yoga for Beginners**. As you learn the poses and strengthen your muscles, you will be able to advance to more challenging classes if you desire. There are classes for all ages and levels, including chair yoga!

Find your pace, find your practice, and watch as your life improves!

COURTNEY COMMENT

Yoga is one of my favorite forms of physical activity. I enjoy a good downward dog and sinking into pigeon, but my favorite classes focus on relaxation.

One such class is restorative yoga, which we lovingly call guided naptime in my home. If you find a studio like mine, you will walk into a restorative yoga class and be greeted by the calmest soul and quietest voice; you're immediately at ease. Their only goal is to help you find ultimate comfort. You'll be instructed to grab many props—bolsters, blankets, eye coverings. The lights will be dimmed and the candles lit. Some quiet instrumental music will fill the air. You might hear a chime. You are guided through a journey of love and support. You awake reinvigorated and leave a new person ready to conquer the world!

If you're anything like me, you struggle giving yourself permission to rest. That's the best part of this type of class. Rest is the goal. Rest is celebrated!

Give yoga a try. Find the studio, app, or video series that works for you. At the very least, it's a great reason to invest in new yoga pants and a mat!

58

Meditate

The research in support of meditation is astounding. Meditation has been a part of religious practices for hundreds of years, but the scientific study is more recent. Studies of fMRIs, which measure brain activity, found that meditation strengthens the parts of the brain responsible for emotional reactivity, concentration, and compassion. It can treat depression and reduce stress by slowing your heart rate and relaxing your body.

Courtney learned about meditation in college and wanted to share it with me. She downloaded an app on my phone called **Calm**, and I did a seven-day free trial of guided meditations. All I had to do was press start and follow the verbal instructions to breathe, visualize, scan my body for tension, watch my thoughts float by, and try other mindfulness techniques for about ten minutes a day. Easy, right? Wrong! It was extremely difficult, just sitting and focusing. But I improved each day, and at the end of the week, I was hooked and able to sit in the present moment more easily. It has been over five years and I still meditate daily.

The more I meditate, the better my physical and mental health have become. My blood pressure and cholesterol levels improved, stress affects me less, I connect better with others, and I get more quality sleep. I used to be extremely impatient; while waiting to be served at a restaurant, I would try to get the attention of every server who walked by. Now, I can sit and enjoy the moment. If I get cut off in traffic, I no longer react. The impact is astounding. I learned acceptance for life as it is, people as they are, and events as they happen. I have a monkey brain, jumping from thought to thought in each moment, but meditation calms my racing mind. Just like Bob Marley said, "The day you stop racing is the day you win the race," and that is exactly what meditation has helped me learn—to stop racing and just be.

You are bigger than your thoughts.

You are bigger than your thoughts, and meditation can teach you how to understand and overcome the unhealthy chatter in your head just like it did for me. The mind-body connection is a very real one, and I hope you can feel that for yourself one day.

I'm not suggesting you take a vow of silence, wear a robe, go on a retreat in India, or any other misconception surrounding meditation. Meditating for as little as two minutes a day can greatly impact your health. Find a meditation practice that works for you.

COURTNEY COMMENT

I introduced my father to the **Calm** app. I loved having a regular meditation practice, but I didn't continue past the free trial. I tried working meditation into my daily schedule to become more mindful many different times, but I just wasn't ready to fully commit. And just like meditation preaches, that's okay. Maybe the right time and situation is just around the corner, or maybe not, but I am open and hopeful that I will bring this amazing practice back into my life.

So, right now, I am downloading a new app, Headspace, and starting their two-week free trial! I can't wait to get my Zen on, and if it sticks, great. If not, I'll try again when I'm ready.

I hope you can give it a try too, and allow yourself the same grace to take it as it comes.

59

Be Open to Therapy

I come from a family that sees therapy as a weakness. Like most families, we had our dysfunction, including alcoholism and mental illness. But because of the stigma of therapy, no one ever discussed or dealt with these issues.

Growing up in this type of environment made it difficult to process and overcome my own problems. It wasn't until my marriage started suffering that I was forced to confront my own family history and try to break the cycle.

It wasn't my idea to go to therapy, and I didn't go easily. It was a very stressful time in our lives. My wife was pregnant with our first child; I worked in sales during the week, and I tended bar on the weekends. At that point, I still believed in the work hard, play hard mentality, and a lot of partying contributed to the overall craziness. I believed I was entitled to stay out late drinking with friends since I was the one bringing home the bacon. Michele didn't agree, and my behavior negatively impacted our relationship.

We all have cycles to break.

My wife no longer wanted to be part of this lifestyle, but I couldn't control my actions; I didn't understand what was fueling my need to let loose after work. Michele insisted we go to couples counseling, and after three sessions, the therapist told me in no uncertain terms that this was not a marriage issue—it was a Gene issue.

I was raised believing you had to be "crazy" to see a therapist, and now I was seeing one weekly. Talk about a blow to the ego! But over time, I learned that therapy could help anyone, even me.

What did I learn? I kept everything bottled up inside until it exploded in unhealthy ways. I had to learn strategies to release the pressure in a positive manner. My therapist helped me confront the past so I could be the man I wanted to be. We worked through my father's alcoholism and death, and my tumultuous relationship with my mother. Understanding my parents' relationship through different eyes helped me heal. I honestly believe my wife and I wouldn't be married today if I had not gone on this counseling journey.

Therapy is a safety net in my life, and I come back to it when I'm struggling. I now know there is no shame in seeking help. In fact, I'm very proud of my new, healthier, more realistic view of therapy. Therapy is different than just talking to a friend because it offers a professional and neutral perspective.

We live in a society that constantly focuses on eating right and exercising to maintain our physical health. However, there is rarely open communication around maintaining our mental health. In fact, I don't think you can have one without the other; the mental dictates the physical and vice versa.

Looking to find your own therapist? Choose wisely! It is important to interview a therapist before setting up an appointment. You can request a short telephone conversation to ensure your potential therapist is a good personal fit. There are many types of therapies depending upon your needs (visit https://www.psychologytoday.com/us/types-of-therapy to learn about the various options). If you are unable to find a therapist that takes your insurance, don't give up! Call your insurance provider to get a comprehensive list of local therapists. Another option is contacting a mental health hotline or finding a support group in your area. There are online resources as well such as the American Psychological Association where you can find providers. Worried you cannot afford therapy? You can meet on a short- or long-term basis depending on your need and financial resources. Some counselors charge clients based upon your income (sliding scale) to make services affordable for all. There are even low cost and free programs offered at community centers, hospitals, schools, and places of worship.

We all have problems. We all have cycles to break. You don't have to go through life feeling inferior, depressed, suicidal, out of control, or afraid. There are many reasons to seek therapy. Don't let the stigma stand in your way to a healthy mind.

COURTNEY COMMENT

Unlike my dad, I come from a family that educated me about mental health and encouraged therapy. Younger generations seem to be moving in this direction. That doesn't mean certain stigmas didn't infiltrate my life or affect me.

The biggest stigma that impacted my treatment was preconceived notions about medication. I have generalized anxiety disorder, mild OCD, and suffer from panic attacks. I was an extremely Type A kid, but my mental health did not become a problem requiring treatment until my early twenties (a common age for mental illness to manifest or intensify).

I began having panic attacks in college and met with a therapist weekly to address the problem using CBT (cognitive behavioral therapy). After one year, she suggested seeing a psychiatrist as well. A psychologist helps you work through problems using any number of methods depending on your diagnosis and provider. You meet regularly with this doctor. A psychiatrist manages and prescribes your medication, and you often meet only a few times a year. The issue for me? My mom was not an advocate of medication because her mother and grandmother were both prescription drug abusers. I didn't want to upset my mom, and I wrongly believed medication meant I was weak and had failed. Regardless, my panic attacks became serious enough that I decided to try it.

My life changed.

I will never forget when my mom visited me shortly after starting anxiety medication. She helped me set up my college room, which usually took hours upon hours of re-centering and moving items around until I felt they were "perfect." This time, when my mom hung a picture that was slightly tilted, I told her not to worry about it. Her jaw just about hit the floor. My medication helped me manage the obsessive thoughts and perfectionism, making them feel less urgent. I finally knew what inner silence felt like. Who I am at the core is the same, but I can now do the work needed to get better. Although I still suffer with my mental health, it's more manageable.

Mental illnesses, now referred to as brain diseases, are chemical imbalances. Medication is not a magic cure-all, but it can help re-balance your brain chemistry. Taking medication has nothing to do with weakness and everything to do with simple biology. When you have strep, you take an antibiotic. When you have anxiety, you can also treat the root cause. Seeing how medication helped me, my mom changed her opinion and now takes an anti-anxiety medication herself. There are medications available for many different mental illnesses, not just anxiety disorders.

My goal is not to promote medication. In fact, you should weigh the pros and cons carefully with a psychiatrist as side effects can be intense and include weight gain, low libido, and stomach upset. Rather, I'm sharing my story so that if this stigma is a roadblock for you or someone you love, you now know there are options.

Looking for help and don't know where to start?
Visit nami.org/home
to find educational resources, support groups, and more.

60

Marry the Right Person

The most important decision of your life is who you marry. It's not a decision to be made lightly—your happiness, or unhappiness, will be largely dictated by this choice.

The American Psychological Association states that 40-50% of first marriages in the United States end in divorce. This shocking statistic is a strong indication that the way in which we perceive marriage and choose a partner needs to be given much more consideration.

It's a lot more painful to live your life trapped in an unhappy marriage than to face a breakup.

How can you be assured that you fall on the successful side of this statistic? Finances, infidelity, lack of commitment, constant arguing, and lack of intimacy are cited as top reasons for divorce. I suggest that you have many serious conversations about these topics before walking down the aisle.

Michele and I attended a premarital weekend retreat (Pre-Cana) through my Catholic church, and it confirmed that we were making the right decision in choosing each other. We participated in a series of activities that prompted us to have many difficult but necessary conversations. My favorite activity included rating our priorities in order of importance and sharing them with each other. Some of the priorities we were asked to consider were work, hobbies and other interests, time alone, time together, children, rest, charity, relatives, religion, friends, household duties, and recreation.

Michele and I were in sync, and when we differed, it was minimal. This confirmed our beliefs in each other and our union. Unfortunately, many of the couples were arguing over each other's rankings: "Why am I always last?" "Why is work most important?" It was sad to hear, but it is necessary information to address as a couple. If we did the exercise again today, we would probably have the same lists because they relate to your values and lifestyle, who you are at the core.

When you become serious with a partner, I suggest you discuss what is most important to each of you. Be honest with each other. If you cannot compromise and accept your partner's point of view, then you might need to be honest with yourself—is this relationship right for you? Trust your gut. It's a lot more painful to live your life trapped in an unhappy marriage than to face a breakup.

What if your partner is committed to making changes to align with your values? Don't marry someone thinking you can change them! If you're waiting until marriage for your partner to become more honest, committed, available, or trustworthy, the likelihood of this happening is very small. It's important to believe in each other completely before you enter into this sacred covenant.

Marriage is hard work. Find the right person, and you can work through all the challenging times together and enjoy one hell of a ride along the way.

COURTNEY COMMENT

I highly recommend that you live with someone before getting married. I know this is uncommon for older generations, but it's the best choice my husband and I ever made. A marriage is a lifetime, and I strongly believe you can't choose to be with someone forever before knowing you can make it through day-to-day life.

The most difficult time in our relationship was when we first moved in together. We had very different lifestyles. Rich needed a lot of alone time, and I wanted to be together constantly. He spent hours playing videogames, and I wanted to get out of the house and take adventures.

There are also the little differences, like how often we ran the dishwasher, picking up hair in the shower, and nighttime routines. The big and the small could have broken us. But instead, we learned together. We compromised. We laughed. We let each other in. We needed this time to either grow together or grow apart before deciding on forever, and I'm so happy we did!

Living together is a true and critical test.

Pictures of the love letters we wrote to each other at Pre-Cana.

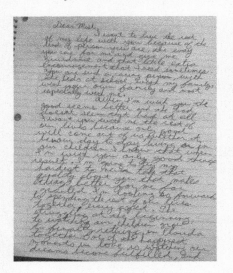

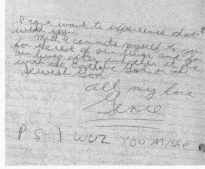

61

Leave Your Baggage Behind

My wife and I damaged our children. Royally. And it's a direct result of our baggage. No book can assure that you will be a perfect parent or partner. We are all human, which means you'll make mistakes, but I truly hope you can learn from ours.

A lot of who you are and how you love comes from your upbringing, which can be helpful or hurtful, or even both at the same time. You come into relationships with a suitcase full of history that impacts how you act as a friend, romantic partner, and possibly one day a parent. The damage that you carry forward into those relationships is what many people refer to as your baggage.

In our case, two of us were parenting together with similar baggage, which exacerbated the hurt we caused our children. The baggage I wish I had understood and addressed earlier in our marriage surrounds food and exercise. Growing up, I was made to clear my plate, and, to this day, I can't eat cooked vegetables because my father physically forced me to swallow them. We never learned about health and nutrition. I was overweight in my twenties, and as a young father, I was often on the road where fast food was king. Then I read a health book and took its advice to the extreme. I started to exercise and eat strictly. I had my children do the same, hoping to teach them the knowledge my parents didn't have to give to me.

Meanwhile, my wife had baggage surrounding eating and exercise, too. She grew up in a family where her father treated her mother and sister horribly because they were overweight, and so they were on and off diets all the time, even attending "fat camps." Her other siblings struggled with eating disorders, and my wife has a history of restrictive eating and obsessive exercising.

Our kids? It was the perfect storm. Even with some awareness, our baggage scarred our children. I think deep down we knew we should leave them alone when it came to diet and exercise. We should have understood intuitive eating and set realistic rather than obsessive examples. We should have taught them that all bodies and foods are valid and lovable. But we couldn't do it, and all four of our children struggle with eating disorders and body image to this day. We didn't break the cycle.

Reflecting back, it's clear how we got here. One moment, I'm reading about the importance of exercise, and in the next I'm obsessing over my son's athletic training. One day, Michele is watching her father berate her mother in disgust over her appearance, and years later, Michele's taking her fourth grader to Weight Watchers. There's a montage that flashes before our eyes with images of a thin Michele claiming she's fat, needing to lose five pounds before a trip, and me, ordering half portions of food while working out twice a day on vacations. In the peripheral of these memories are our children witnessing all these extreme behaviors.

The montage transforms into images of our elementary-aged kids counting out a serving size of SnackWell's cookies, tracking their number of workouts a week, and sneaking food into their rooms. We made too many rules and focused too much on weight. It got out of control, and we were poor role models. At mealtime, Michele would noticeably look at our kids with disdain—she carried their pictures in her purse and put an X on the photos each time she caught herself staring in disgust as a reminder of the harm she was doing. By that point, we were already working to do better, but the damage was done.

All we wanted to do was help our children. We thought we were teaching them how to maintain a healthy weight and exercise routine, but it had the opposite impact. This is a heavy burden we now carry for the rest of our lives.

If we had accepted and dealt with our demons and focused more on discarding the baggage we brought into our marriage, perhaps the outcome would have been different. It is a challenge our children are working to overcome with our grandchildren.

When you recognize and repair your past, you leave the baggage behind and free up space to love unconditionally.

What baggage do you carry? Identify it; accept it; understand it; commit to changing it. And do it sooner rather than later. As you become more aware, you will be a better partner and person. When you recognize and repair your past, you leave the baggage behind and free up space to love unconditionally. Use our tale as a cautionary one, and break the cycle for future generations.

COURTNEY COMMENT

Hello! Damaged Daughter here. Taking ownership and setting boundaries have been a large part of my healing process.

Yes, my parents did some harm. As I mentioned previously, I struggled with obsessive exercise and stringent eating for years, and now I struggle with binge eating disorder. But I don't hate my parents. They did the best they could. I'm an adult who needs to take responsibility for my problems. Their baggage is now my life, and it is mine to heal. It's my turn to break the cycle, and I'm working on that for my family.

Setting boundaries is an extremely healthy part of that process. I have identified my triggers and used them to decide what limits I have when it comes to my parents. I have communicated that my body, diet, and exercise are not theirs to discuss. I have made it clear that these subjects should not be brought up. Luckily, they respect that boundary.

I encourage you to do the same (beware: it's much harder than it looks). Understand your limits with those who have hurt you and protect those boundaries so that you can heal. At the same time, let go of the blame and hatred toward others who may have hurt you. Anger and resentment will not get you anywhere. You too are an adult, and it is now your hurt to repair. Your loved ones are depending on it (maybe you can check out that "Be Open to Therapy" chapter again!).

Sincerely,

Healing Adult

62

When You Lose It, You Lose

It's easy to lose your temper and hard to control it. I'm here to remind you of what you already know but might struggle to do—keep your anger in check. When you lose it, you lose.

Growing up, there was a lot of yelling and turmoil in my house. My parents raised their voices often and there was physical violence as well. When I became a father, I knew I needed a different way to handle my rage. This awareness helped me in all my relationships. Whether it's your intimate relationships, your professional ones, or your friendships, there is always a better way to react than with anger.

The opposite of reactivity is mindfulness.

I had three daughters in their teens at the same time and a son watching my every move, so I had to consciously choose calm over chaos. I became incredibly good at keeping my cool. When my oldest daughter drove her car into a ditch outside a police station, I stayed calm and collected. When my middle daughter lost my keys on an airplane and we landed late at night with a puppy and no ride home, I breathed through it and called a cab. When my youngest daughter, Courtney, backed into a parked jeep mere days after purchasing her new car, I didn't lose it. Through fights over clothes, toys, and TV time, I kept my head on straight.

But there was a time my emotions got the best of me during these chaotic years. I still cringe when I think about it. One of my daughters was being very disrespectful and would not get off the computer. I completely lost it. I yelled. And when she wouldn't move, I physically pulled her up the stairs toward her room. Later, I felt disgusted with myself. Was I right asking her to be respectful and leave the computer to help clean up? Of course! Often, parents are right. Does that matter? Not at all. Once I lost it, the only message received was that her dad was a jerk. Was she thinking about her missteps? Of course not. She was feeling afraid of her father and even angrier than before. And I was sending the message to all my children that it is okay to become physical when you are angry.

It is never productive or responsible to handle stress by lashing out. Even if you are "right," the second you raise your voice, you become wrong. It is also embarrassing to yourself and others when you lose control. You are not thinking straight in those moments. You become driven by emotion rather than rationality. Biologically, when you're angry, you release stress hormones, and the sensible part of your brain shuts down.

So how do you resist those primal urges and stay calm when anger swells? Take time to stop and think before reacting. The opposite of reactivity is mindfulness. Walk away and identify what's really driving your anger. What's the root of the problem? Yelling won't solve it, so figure out what will. Give yourself time to cool off and let the rational part of your brain re-engage. It's not easy in the moment, but you must take a step back.

Reacting impulsively with anger will slowly damage your relationships. When you're angry and fighting, you talk over each other and focus on how to win the argument rather than on listening, understanding, and resolving. Eventually, you may stop communicating altogether. You will never deal with the core of your issues if all you do is put out fires. It's important for you and the people you love to resolve conflicts calmly. Do all you can to keep your anger in check. That's when you really win.

COURTNEY COMMENT

As a young wife, I often need to remind myself not to lose it. It still happens, but it never brings about the outcome I want.

When I'm angry, I say hurtful things. Those words are often hard to forget for the other person. They linger and can't be taken back. What has helped my marriage is taking a "cool-off" period before working on resolving an issue (which allows us to talk rather than fight). This pause allows me to evaluate the situation and understand what is happening beneath the surface.

The same advice is helpful in your professional life. Do not respond to emails when you're angry! Wait a day. This has saved my career many times. Nothing good comes when anger takes over.

63

Schedule Date Nights

Never stop dating!

As your romantic relationship progresses, it's easy for life to get in the way. Work, bills, the gym, kids—there's so much going on that seems to take precedent. Your foundation is strong, so what's the worst a little neglect could do?

A lot. What happens when weeks, or even months, go by without quality time together (no, sleeping doesn't count)? Eventually, it becomes your new normal. Before you know it, years have passed, and you can't remember the last time you went on a date, or what brought you together in the first place.

The solution? Date night! Michele started the tradition of a weekly date night when I was working crazy hours in corporate America. Although we had little money to spare, we scheduled a sitter for every Wednesday night so we could go out as a couple. We did something as simple as the diner or a quick movie, but we were together. Nothing could interfere with this routine, and it became a sacred, protected part of our week. I recently reconnected with a former colleague, Lloyd, who laughed when remembering that on Wednesdays there was no way to get me to stay late—it was my date night, and everyone knew.

**Your relationship deserves to be
protected and prioritized.**

As our lives became busier, our weekly reprieve became more and more vital. With four young kids, schedules went to a new level of crazy. But one night a week we reconnected, really talked and listened, and simply had fun. It was a regular reminder of why we fell in love. Your relationship deserves to be protected and prioritized. Date night will help you and your partner increase intimacy, release stress, communicate better, and rekindle your spark.

What does date night look like? If money is tight, you can simply go for a walk. If you cannot afford, find, or trust a babysitter, see if there is a friend or family member who will help you for an hour so you can get out. Just sixty minutes can be more than enough time. If children are not in your plan, time with your partner is still essential. Work and other commitments are just as distracting.

Stuck in a rut? Put some date night ideas in a jar and pick from there. It could be a date morning, afternoon, or happy hour! The possibilities are endless if you remain open.

Unique Date Ideas

- Picnic
- Mini-Golf
- Board Game
- Puzzle or Lego
- Make Your Own Pizza
- Live Music
- Batting Cages
- Sing (or laugh at) Karaoke
- Flea Market
- Road Trip
- Trivia Night
- Bike Ride
- Brewery
- Wildlife Refuge
- Local Groupon Deals

Your connection may be the most important aspect of your marriage; without it, you lose your foundation. You and your partner deserve uninterrupted time. It takes effort, but so do many of the things that bring us joy. If you lose your bond, what are you left with?

COURTNEY COMMENT

I love the challenge of finding a new and different date night idea.

My husband and I once did a Barnes and Noble scavenger hunt to get out but not spend any money. We put our phones away and split up to find books to bring back to the other based upon a prompt like, "Find a cookbook with a recipe you'd like us to try" or "What was your favorite book as a child?" I learned his was *Oh, The Places You'll Go!* by Dr. Seuss and took a mental note to get it for him when we had our first baby. That night, we laughed so hard and learned so much about each other. We were both very present.

These are the times that keep your love growing.

64

Respect Your In-Laws

When you commit to your partner, you also commit to their family. Just as you respect your parents, you should respect your in-laws and go out of your way to make them feel part of your lives.

**When you honor your in-laws,
you honor your partner.**

Until my mother-in-law passed away, I sent her flowers each year on my wife's birthday. I sent her yellow roses (her favorite) with a note thanking her for giving birth to the love of my life on that day years ago. She appreciated this gesture, but I never understood how much it meant to her until we sat shiva after her funeral. A group of her friends asked me if I was the son-in-law who sent the yellow roses. They told me that she always bragged about her flowers and that she loved me very much. The flowers were a small gesture, but they made a big impact. I encourage you to steal this idea, too!

Most importantly, my wife appreciated that I went out of my way to make her mom feel special. When you honor your in-laws, you honor your partner.

It is even more important to make an effort to nurture relationships with your in-laws when you do not live in close proximity. My daughter Shannon and her family moved to the Philadelphia area for work. Her in-laws reside in Rhode Island, and she does a wonderful job of staying connected. Shannon prioritizes visiting them for holidays, especially those that are important to her husband like the Fourth of July. They call her in-laws often and plan vacations together. She talks to her children about her husband's parents. Physical distance can be taxing, but your effort will go a long way.

Many people struggle with their relationships with their in-laws. Combining families brings challenges. It's okay to set boundaries when needed. You should also work hard to accept your new family and create positive experiences, especially when it's important to your spouse. This includes their siblings as well. Can you give them a special role in planning a family event? Is there an activity you could do together to create a positive memory? What matters to your partner's family? How can you participate in and support that? Learn their traditions, listen to their stories, and make time for them. Consider sending a text message to thank them for something. Offer help. Treat them the way you wish your family to be treated. It might not always be easy, but it is important.

COURTNEY COMMENT

What if your in-laws are extremely difficult people? Think Marie from *Everybody Loves Raymond* or Jack in *Meet the Fockers*.

Do you give up? Give in?

There is a difference between giving up and giving in. You do not have to give up on a relationship with your in-laws, but you also don't have to give in to their chaos. It is important to, once again, set boundaries that are healthy for you and your family. The way you wish to run your home takes precedence over their opinions.

If your mother-in-law, for example, tries to tell you to feed your baby solids before you are ready, you can decline and explain your feelings. Respect does not mean blind compliance. If she is angry with you or tries to overstep, you need to stand your ground.

It is imperative that you and your partner are on the same page about the boundaries you set. If they cannot openly support you, you will never succeed with their family.

Beyond boundary setting, it might give you clarity to consider why your in-laws are behaving as they are. This does not excuse their actions, but it might help you approach them with a bit more empathy. Empathy is helpful because the more you can deescalate the situation and stay calm, the more successful you will be.

Respecting difficult in-laws takes work, but consistency can help you reach a place of equilibrium. Unfortunately, people don't often change. So, if your boundaries aren't working and it becomes too toxic, you can always take a break from the relationship to prioritize your health.

65

Be Generous with Time, Praise, and Encouragement

All fulfilling relationships need nurturing. Often, the more tenured a relationship, the less time and effort people spend building up their partner. As time progresses, it might seem unnecessary to share sentiments aloud. You know your partner loves you and appreciates you without them voicing it, but does that mean they should stop saying it? Or showing it?

It is even more important to fuel the fire of your relationships with praise and encouragement as time progresses.

No! It's even more important to fuel the fire of your relationships with praise and encouragement as time progresses. This is when it's easiest to forget the spark that brought you together. Do not allow it to fade.

This goes for all relationships (call your parents up today and tell them you love them; send a friend a text of appreciation), especially intimate ones. When it comes to your partner, don't be afraid to show affection. Hold hands when talking, use terms of endearment, express your love verbally, and give hugs. Michele and I have made it a ritual to give each other a kiss and say "I love you" every night before falling asleep.

Another way to show affection is to write a "just because" note or card. Michele and I each have one note from the other hanging in our closet as a constant reminder of our love and acceptance for each other. Michele has even framed some of these notes. The note can be simple: "I'm heading out for coffee and wanted to tell you how beautiful you are." The main idea is to remind your partner that you are thinking of them. A text or an email can accomplish this too.

Make sure your appreciation and praise are genuine. Give sincere compliments often. They can be simple: "Breakfast was great today," or "Your outfit looks really nice."

Your partner might *know* deep down they are loved, but hearing it frequently and expressing it regularly helps to keep that love and positivity on the forefront. This goes for any relationship you have—tend to it and it will keep growing!

This is especially important and difficult advice to remember when in a dispute. It is most important to be gentle then. A disagreement is not a fight. If you approach a dispute like a battle, you assume there's a winner and a loser. In relationships, there's neither. You're on the same team.

It's okay to give in. Acquiescing is an act of love, not surrender. When arguments arise, it's never a win-lose situation when you make someone you care about happy. Especially when they do the same for you. That's love, not war. Work to intentionally bring love, praise, and affection to every day.

COURTNEY COMMENT

Consider your love languages. Author Gary Chapman outlines five ways people give and receive love. Understanding your partner's preferences will help you understand where to focus your energy when giving time, praise, and encouragement.

Love Languages

1. Words of Affirmation: You feel most loved when given compliments from your partner.
2. Quality Time: You feel most loved when you spend uninterrupted time with your partner.
3. Acts of Service: You feel most loved when your partner does deeds for you, such as taking out the trash or brushing snow off your car.
4. Receiving Gifts: You feel most loved when you receive a present from your partner.
5. Physical Touch: You feel most loved through touch—hugs, kisses, cuddles, handholding.

Know what works for your relationship and show love appropriately! For me, all my husband needs to do is give a compliment and I am putty in his arms. For him? Bake him brownies or walk the dog and he's falling in love all over again!

66

Share the Financial Details

Finances are a leading cause of divorce. I always worry when a young married couple keep their money separate. It is a formula for failure, as separate is often synonymous with secret. Why hide something from your partner? When you marry, you join in a union that includes your money and what you do with it.

**What is important is that you agree on your fiscal roles
and keep each other in the loop.**

I challenge you to be open and honest with your partner about your financial situation before you get married. Share your debt, your savings, your salary, your earning potential, and your general feelings about money. If you hide any financial detail, you could create unrealistic expectations and foster mistrust. Be vulnerable and lay it all out on the table. Once you're married, it belongs to both of you.

When Michele and I first married and joined finances, we often argued because I watched every dime while she spent freely. It set up a dynamic where I was a dictator watching over her every move, and that's just too controlling. Trust your partner to make the right decisions and get on the same page about what those decisions look like. I suggest budgeting a small amount for each of you to spend without restriction. When Michele and I did this, it erased unnecessary conflict and feelings of resentment. You shouldn't have to ask permission to stop at Starbucks or buy your sibling a gift. It might be helpful to pick a limit, and if either one of you wants to make a purchase over that amount, you can discuss it first.

Defining financial roles is also helpful. Who will manage the financial accounts? Who will pay what bills? Who will invest your savings? This was easy for Michele and me because I was used to tracking a budget and net worth, and she was on top of the monthly bills. She didn't want to see our accounts and investments regularly. If you are like Michele and me and your roles are obvious, it's still important to share all the financial details with the partner not managing the big-picture money. We decide together how much each of us needs monthly and put that money in a separate account, and then we reassess when necessary.

I share all our financial information annually, so she has it. Every New Year's Eve, I write her a note outlining where all our money is located, what's in each account, contact information for investors, our lawyer, and our accountant, and updated log-in information. We are in this together, and if anything ever happens to me, she has all the information she needs.

When we first married, Michele was a speech therapist, but we decided together we wanted her to stay home with our kids if we could afford it (Michele always said she was ready to go back to work if needed). When one person takes on the responsibility of the family and the other the earnings, it can create a fissure in the relationship, especially if the at-home partner is not trusted with the financial details. If you decide as a couple that one of you will stay home, it is a family decision. The money earned by one is as much the other partner's money (just as the kids are equally both yours). And it's the working partner's job to make their spouse feel that sentiment.

When both spouses work, usually one still prefers to manage the money, and you must share everything in that situation as well. If both partners want to manage the finances, you can split tasks and check-in on the big picture monthly. Sharing the responsibility is made easier if you have a clear budget and delegation of duties. If no one wants to manage the finances, then you will have to come together and figure that out. What is important is that you agree on your fiscal roles and keep each other in the loop.

What works for one couple might not work for another. Find your own formula and define your roles. Most importantly, be honest and open, and never forget you're on the same team.

COURTNEY COMMENT

I have seen many people try to hide fiscal missteps from their partners out of shame. I think men, especially, carry an unrealistic and outdated burden of being the breadwinners. There seems to be an immense sense of responsibility to carry that burden alone.

I am here to say, to shout, WISE UP! Put your ego aside and let your partner help. Lose your job? Tell your partner and get through it together! Believe me, hiding it so they "don't have to worry" only makes it worse in the end. Behind on mortgage payments? Make a plan as a couple! It's the twenty-first century, and you are not in this alone.

Maybe that means deciding one person gets a second job, or you take a penalty and borrow against your 401(k). Regardless, make those decisions as a team.

67

Create, Adopt, and Honor Family Traditions

Traditions are the cornerstone of the family. My favorite family tradition is our holiday notes, and I encourage you to steal this idea just like we did.

Every Christmas Eve, Michele and I write a note to each other reflecting on the year. Our children joined as soon as they could draw. We have thirty-eight years of notes that we read over various days during the holiday season. Reliving our beautiful, messy life together brings tears, laughter, and reflection as we remember those we've lost and the special moments of our lives.

I cringe when I look at my first notes; they were short with very little introspection. But then again, these differences show me how much I've grown as a husband, father, and human being. Now, I write smaller and smaller each year to fit as much as I can to stay within our "rule" of only one small piece of paper per person. This most beloved tradition has become a permanent piece of our family history for generations to come (yes, we've even included these notes in our will).

Whether or not you embrace holiday notes, I encourage you to establish your own family traditions. There are many benefits—creating strong bonds with the people you love, teaching your family history, reinforcing your values, creating lasting memories, and keeping your culture alive.

Traditions are the cornerstone of the family.

Michele and I attended a college graduation party for a young man I mentored. He is Igbo, from western Nigeria. The presentation of the kola nut is a tradition they embrace to keep their culture at the heart of their celebrations. It is a way to welcome their guests and begin the festivities. The kola nut is very special to the Igbo people and represents peace and friendship. I was honored to be invited as one of the four men participating in the kola nut ceremony, where an elder prayed over the nut and then we ate it. I loved learning about their traditions and even more so seeing how it connects their family together through generations.

Your tradition might be Sunday night dinners, annual beach vacations, game night, or pizza Fridays. Whatever your tradition may be, it will strengthen your bond and create lasting memories.

Year 1 Vs.

with him SHAN + DOUG CONTINUE to share their CHildren with us every Wed + MONDAY. I know we both feel this is our greatest gift + JOY. We ACtUALLY grew tomatoes this year with Dylan + Emmy. We continue to give back with PAS AND have met some Amazing Kids + parents as a result. Our Kenz Continues on her Journey and 2019 has seen us attend NAR-ANON meetings AND FINALLY ALLows us to grasp the severity of her problems. We Lost LILLY After 24 years which Allowed her to grow. My Brother Brian's house (the house I grew up in) burned down to the ground but everyone was safe and he will get A brand New home. We had an amazing time in the Azores, Nashville and ocean City this year. I do not know what's in store for us in 2020 but I know with you by my side we will figure it out + ALways be okay!

Year 36

COURTNEY COMMENT

Speaking of my parents' will, we all have different responsibilities. My oldest sister is the executor, my middle sister is responsible for the beach house, my brother will financially manage our family charitable trust, and me? I am the keeper of the notes and journals. Yup, you read that right...

My dad keeps telling me it's the most valuable thing he has, but I'll let you be the judge of that.

In all seriousness, I am honored to pass these stories down for generations to come! Holiday notes are also one of my most treasured traditions. I now write them with my husband and son, but I do sometimes break the "one-page rule."

68

Prepare Your Will

As many as 60% of U.S. adults do not have a will. They either never get around to making it, find it difficult to face their mortality, or believe they have nothing of importance to legally delegate. Living in a post-pandemic world is a good reminder that life is short, and you are never too young to get your affairs in order.

Preparing a will is an act of love. I highly recommend using a lawyer to guide you through this process. You can find a template online and write your own will, but especially as you grow older and have more accounts, assets, and need for estate planning, you'll benefit from an expert's help. When completed, you sign and date it, have two witnesses also sign, and name an executor (the person that will carry out the terms of your will upon your death), and the document is legal.

The most important items to include in a will are:

- **Beneficiaries:** Those who will inherit your assets
- **Assets:** Anything you own (e.g., house, car, business, jewelry, heirlooms)
- **Debts:** Any money you owe (e.g., mortgage, credit cards, loans, taxes)

- **Guardians:** Those who will take guardianship of your pets or children if they are under eighteen and the other parent is also deceased
- **Executor:** The person in charge of enacting your will

Wills should be:

- Specific
- Signed and dated
- Safely stored
- Updated regularly
- Discussed with the beneficiaries and executor ASAP

I was the executor for my favorite uncle's estate, and I learned a lot from the process. He had four children, and no matter how hard I tried, the siblings no longer speak to each other because of how the will was prepared. I have heard too many stories of families falling apart after a parent passes away because they feel they are not being treated fairly or someone takes items another believes aren't theirs to take. To avoid this situation, you must have a clear will and communicate your wishes while you're still alive.

**Life is short and you are never too young
to get your affairs in order.**

How clear should you be? Determine how your assets will be divided and try to keep it as simple as possible. When both my wife and I are gone, our will specifies that everything should be sold and divided equally four ways. We also outlined specific responsibilities for each of our four children and described how to divide or sell heirlooms. Make sure you are specific about roles and explain how you want the nostalgic items divided to avoid possible family conflict.

There is also a document referred to as a living will that you can prepare to specify your medical treatment in the case you cannot make those decisions for yourself. You can dictate a person to make the choices for you, called your power of attorney, and you can detail preferences such as a DNR (do not resuscitate), comfort care, dialysis, and donating your organs. Making these decisions ahead of time cements your wishes and takes the pressure and responsibility off your loved ones.

As far as communicating these decisions, I suggest making time for a family discussion and keep it as unemotional as possible so you can be clear and answer all questions. Our kids jokingly called this the "death talk," and we recorded the discussion to make sure nothing could be misconstrued. You should take this opportunity to make it clear that your final wish is for them to protect their relationships above all else.

The assets you leave behind are surely significant, but what will be remembered the most are your words. My final and most important piece of advice is to leave behind letters and/or a video for your loved ones. My mother-in-law wrote a personal note to her spouse and each of her children that she kept in a safe. The letters were thirty years old when she passed, and they meant so much more to her family than any of her material possessions. Michele and I have written letters to our children and children in-law so they will have the same gift.

When preparing your will, ask yourself what you want to leave behind and how you want to be remembered. You will make mistakes, but if you learn from them, you will be proud of the legacy you created. Finishing this book is a step in that journey, and the person standing at the end of the road will be one incredible human being!

COURTNEY COMMENT

I'm not crying—you're crying! I don't want to think about the day I get those letters.

My parents remind us often that they never want my siblings and me to have conflict over their will. It would dishonor the lives they lived. I really do believe my parents will haunt me from the grave if we mess this one up!

As we arrive at the last chapter of the book, what better way to leave you than with the last chapter of your life? What I hope this book has given you are tools for living a life that makes you proud, a life that fuels your passions, a life that leaves a positive influence on the world, a life of meaning. Then, when the day comes to enact your will (hopefully many well-lived years from now), that document will be the least important thing you're passing on. It will be your memories, your joy, and your impact that are your legacy.

Thank you for opening your mind and heart to our stories and advice. I wish you many, many blessings and a life of true fulfillment.

FINAL THOUGHTS

**Success is not final, failure is not fatal:
it is the courage to continue that counts."**

—WINSTON CHURCHILL

We appreciate you, our readers, for investing your time in this book. We sincerely hope that whatever your next steps are in life, you feel more prepared and inspired. As Churchill reminds us, there will be highs and lows in your journey, but "it is the courage to continue that counts." Always keep moving forward and never take success for granted.

Use these tools. Follow your passions and remember your foundation; they are your core. Protect them and honor them. You deserve the future of your dreams. It's within your reach. You are capable and you are ready—now go out and get it!